FOOD EDITOR: Pamela Clark

ASSISTANT FOOD EDITORS: Kathy McGarry,
Louise Patniotis

ASSOCIATE FOOD EDITORS: Karen Hammial,
Lucy Kelly

HOME ECONOMISTS: Emma Braz, Nadia French,
Justin Kerr, Maria Sampsonis, Jodie Tilse, Amal Webster,
Lovoni Welch

EDITORIAL COORDINATOR: Elizabeth Hooper

KITCHEN ASSISTANT: Amy Wong

STYLISTS: Carolyn Fienberg, Kay Francis, Jane Hann,
Cherise Koch, Sophia Young

PHOTOGRAPHERS: Robert Clark, Robert Taylor

■ ■ ■

ART DIRECTOR: Sue de Guingand

ARTIST: Annemarlene Hissink

■ ■ ■

HOME LIBRARY STAFF

EDITOR-IN-CHIEF: Mary Coleman

ASSISTANT EDITORS:
Mary-Anne Danaher, Lynne Testoni

SUB-EDITOR: Brenda Christian

EDITORIAL COORDINATOR: Lee Stephenson

■ ■ ■

MANAGING DIRECTOR: Colin Morrison

GROUP PUBLISHER: Tim Trumper

CIRCULATION & MARKETING DIRECTOR:
Chris Gibson

■ ■ ■

Produced by The Australian Women's Weekly Home Library.
Colour separations by ACP Colour Graphics Pty Ltd., Sydney.
Printing by Hannanprint, Sydney.
Published by ACP Publishing Pty. Limited, 54 Park Street,
Sydney; GPO Box 4088, Sydney, NSW 1028, (02) 282 8000.
◆ AUSTRALIA: Distributed by Network Distribution
Company, 54 Park Street, Sydney, (02) 9282 8777.
◆ UNITED KINGDOM: Distributed in the U.K. by Australian
Consolidated Press (UK) Ltd, 20 Galowhill Rd, Brackmills,
Northampton NN4 7EE, (01604) 760 456.
◆ CANADA: Distributed in Canada by Whitecap Books Ltd,
351 Lynn Ave, North Vancouver, B.C. V7J 2C4, (604) 980 9852.
◆ NEW ZEALAND: Distributed in New Zealand by Netlink
Distribution Company, 17B Hargreaves St, Level 5,
College Hill, Auckland 1, (9) 302 7616.
◆ SOUTH AFRICA: Distributed in South Africa by Intermag,
PO Box 57394, Springfield 2137, Johannesburg, (011) 491 7534.

■ ■ ■

The Great Beef Cookbook
Includes index.
ISBN 1 86396 055 4

1.Cookery (Beef). Title: Australian
Women's Weekly. (Series: Australian
Women's Weekly Home Library).

641.662

■ ■ ■

© A C P Publishing Pty. Limited 1997
ACN 053 273 546
◆ This publication is copyright. No part of it may be
reproduced or transmitted in any form without the
written permission of the publishers.

■ ■ ■

COVER: Mediterranean Steak Towers, page 30.
Plate and jug from Accoutrement.
LEFT: Aussie Meat Pies, page 85.
BACK COVER: Marinated Beef with Peanuts
and Vegetables, page 7.
Bowl from Made in Japan; box from Bayteak Leisure Store.
RIGHT: Kashmiri Meatballs with Spinach Raita, page 34.

■ ■ ■

The Great Beef Cookbook

From family favourites to classic European dishes, from quick and tasty contemporary stir-fries to long-simmering stews and casseroles, no meat offers as many possibilities to the cook as does beef. Here are more than 150 recipes, new twists on great classics and inventive, quick and easy ideas that every busy cook will love. There's even a section on beef in the microwave, plus suggestions for sauces and butters that highlight the meat's fabulous flavour. In addition to a glossary that defines relevant cooking terms and techniques, The Great Beef Cookbook includes both a complete guide to buying, storing and preparing various cuts, and the officially recognised beef-cuts chart.

FOOD EDITOR

BRITISH & NORTH AMERICAN READERS:
Please note that Australian cup and
spoon measurements are metric. A quick
conversion guide appears on page 127.
A glossary explaining unfamiliar terms
and ingredients appears on page 120.

Contents

Tartare of Beef with Caper Mayonnaise, page 14.

Beef Ragout, page 54.

Beef and Reef, page 26.

Beef Rib Roast with Garlic Herb Butter, page 65.

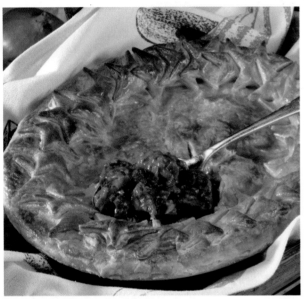
Steak and Kidney Pie, page 74.

Gingered Beef and Coconut Soup, page 23.

The *Famous* Test Kitchen

Pamela Clark, pictured above centre, with three of the Home Economists from the Test Kitchen.

*S*ince 1976, The Australian Women's Weekly Home Library Test Kitchen has researched, tested, photographed and produced more than 70 full-length cookbooks which have combined sales of over 30 million copies, published into 18 different languages, worldwide.

Food Editor Pamela Clark and a staff of home economists create every recipe, then triple-test each one for guaranteed success, ease of preparation, accessibility of ingredients... and great taste.

Quick & Easy

Here are more than 50 beef recipes that busy cooks will love – from quick and tasty contemporary stir-fries, sizzling steaks, and hearty soups to spicy kebabs and a selection of delicious veal dishes. There's a fuss-free recipe to suit every occasion and all can be prepared quickly and easily.

CHAR-GRILLED VEAL SALAD

¼ cup (60ml) olive oil
1 teaspoon chilli flakes
2 tablespoons lemon juice
2 (660g) veal fillets
1 bunch (120g) rocket
250g cherry tomatoes, halved
125g snow peas, thinly sliced
1 small (150g) yellow
    capsicum, sliced
½ cup (40g) flaked
    parmesan cheese

PESTO DRESSING
⅓ cup (80ml) pesto
¼ cup (60ml) olive oil
1½ tablespoons white
    wine vinegar
1 teaspoon sugar

Combine oil, chilli, juice and fillets in large bowl; cover, refrigerate about 6 hours or overnight.

Drain fillets; cook in heated oiled griddle pan (or grill or barbecue) until well browned both sides and cooked as desired. Remove from pan, cover; stand 5 minutes. Slice fillets thinly.

Combine slices with torn rocket, tomatoes, snow peas, capsicum and parmesan in large bowl. Pour Pesto Dressing over, toss gently to combine.
Pesto Dressing: Whisk all ingredients together in bowl.

Serves 4 to 6.

■ Best prepared a day ahead.
■ Storage: Covered, in refrigerator.
■ Freeze: Uncooked marinated fillets suitable.
■ Microwave: Not suitable.

Picnic rug from Bondi Storehouse

SPICED VEAL CUTLETS WITH CORIANDER RAITA

1/4 cup (60ml) yogurt
1 teaspoon grated lemon rind
1 tablespoon lemon juice
1 tablespoon tandoori paste
8 (1kg) veal cutlets

CORIANDER RAITA
1 cup (250ml) yogurt
2 small (260g) Lebanese cucumbers, seeded, chopped
1 large (250g) tomato, seeded, chopped
1 teaspoon ground cumin
1 tablespoon lemon juice
1 tablespoon chopped fresh coriander leaves

Combine yogurt, rind, juice, paste and cutlets in large bowl; cover, refrigerate 3 hours or overnight.

Drain cutlets; cook, in batches, in heated oiled griddle pan (or grill or barbecue) until browned both sides and cooked as desired. Serve cutlets with Coriander Raita.

Coriander Raita: Place all ingredients in small bowl; stir until combined.

Serves 4 to 6.

■ Cutlets best prepared a day ahead. Coriander Raita best made just before serving.
■ Storage: Cutlets, covered, in refrigerator.
■ Freeze: Not suitable.
■ Microwave: Not suitable.

MARINATED BEEF WITH PEANUTS AND VEGETABLES

Beef strips can be prepared from blade, fillet, rib eye, round, rump, sirloin or topside. We used South Cape stir-fry noodles in this recipe; hokkien or rice noodles can be substituted.

750g beef strips
2 tablespoons chopped fresh lemon grass
2 tablespoons lime juice
1/4 cup chopped fresh coriander leaves
1 tablespoon fish sauce
1/4 cup (60ml) mild sweet chilli sauce
2 teaspoons grated fresh ginger
2 cloves garlic, crushed
1 bunch (400g) baby carrots, halved
150g sugar snap peas
500g stir-fry noodles
2 tablespoons peanut oil
1/3 cup (50g) roasted unsalted peanuts, finely chopped

Combine beef strips with lemon grass, juice, coriander, sauces, ginger and garlic in medium bowl; cover, refrigerate 3 hours or overnight.

Boil, steam or microwave carrots and peas, separately, until just tender; drain. Place noodles in large bowl, cover with boiling water, stand for 5 minutes; drain, separate noodles. Heat oil in wok or large pan; stir-fry beef mixture, in batches, until browned and almost cooked. Return beef to wok with carrots, peas, noodles and nuts; stir-fry until heated through.

Serves 4 to 6.

■ Best made just before serving.
■ Freeze: Not suitable.
■ Microwave: Not suitable.

Bowl from Made in Japan, box from Bayteak Leisure Store

OPPOSITE: Spiced Veal Cutlets with Coriander Raita.
ABOVE: Marinated Beef with Peanuts and Vegetables.

Plate from David Jones, Chatswood

STEAKS IN MUSHROOM AND RED WINE SAUCE

Beef rib eye, boneless sirloin or rump steak are also suitable for this recipe.

4 (600g) beef eye fillet steaks
1 tablespoon olive oil
400g Swiss brown mushrooms, sliced
2 cloves garlic, crushed
1 tablespoon tomato paste
1 tablespoon chopped fresh sage leaves
1 teaspoon Dijon mustard
½ cup (125ml) dry red wine
1 cup (250ml) beef stock
½ teaspoon sugar
3 teaspoons cornflour
3 teaspoons water

Tie steaks into rounds with string to hold shape. Heat oil in large pan, add steaks; cook until browned both sides and cooked as desired. Remove from pan, discard string; cover steaks to keep warm.

Add mushrooms and garlic to same pan; cook until mushrooms are soft. Add paste, sage, mustard, wine, stock and sugar; simmer, uncovered, for 5 minutes. Stir in blended cornflour and water; cook, stirring, until mixture boils and thickens. Serve over steaks.

Serves 4.
■ Best made just before serving.
■ Freeze: Not suitable.
■ Microwave: Not suitable.

PEPPER STEAKS IN BRANDY CREAM SAUCE

Boneless sirloin steak is also known as New York cut.

⅓ cup (40g) cracked black peppercorns
3 cloves garlic, crushed
6 (1.2kg) boneless beef sirloin steaks
2 tablespoons olive oil
2 tablespoons brandy
1¼ cups (300ml) cream
½ teaspoon beef stock powder

Combine peppercorns and garlic in small bowl; press mixture over both sides of steaks. Heat oil in large pan; cook steaks, in batches, until browned both sides and cooked as desired. Remove from pan, cover to keep warm; discard burnt peppercorns from pan.

Add brandy to same pan; simmer, stirring, until almost all brandy is evaporated. Add cream and stock powder; simmer, uncovered, about 3 minutes or until the mixture thickens slightly; serve over steaks.

Serves 6.
■ Best made just before serving.
■ Freeze: Not suitable.
■ Microwave: Not suitable.

ABOVE: Steaks in Mushroom and Red Wine Sauce.
OPPOSITE: Pepper Steaks in Brandy Cream Sauce.

Plate from Villeroy & Boch; placemats from Home and Garden on the Mall

BEEF AND HALOUMI KEBABS

Soak bamboo skewers in water overnight to prevent burning.

1kg beef rump steak
350g haloumi cheese
1 tablespoon chopped fresh
thyme leaves
¼ cup chopped fresh mint leaves
2 cloves garlic, crushed
¼ cup (60ml) lemon juice
⅓ cup (80ml) olive oil
1 tablespoon olive oil, extra

Cut steak and haloumi into 2cm cubes, then halve cheese cubes. Thread steak and haloumi alternately on skewers; place in large shallow dish. Combine thyme, mint, garlic, juice and oil in jug, pour over kebabs; cover, refrigerate 3 hours or overnight.

Heat extra oil in large pan; cook kebabs, in batches, until browned all over and cooked as desired.

Serves 4 to 6.

■ Best prepared a day ahead.
■ Storage: Covered, in refrigerator.
■ Freeze: Not suitable.
■ Microwave: Not suitable.

VEAL CUTLETS WITH CHICKPEA AND TOMATO SALAD

8 (1kg) veal cutlets
1 teaspoon ground coriander
1 teaspoon ground cumin
¼ teaspoon chilli powder
2 teaspoons grated lemon rind
1 tablespoon oil

CHICKPEA AND TOMATO SALAD
300g can chickpeas, drained
2 large (500g) tomatoes,
seeded, chopped
1 small (100g) red onion, chopped
2 green onions, finely chopped
2 tablespoons chopped fresh
coriander leaves
1 tablespoon chopped fresh
mint leaves
1 teaspoon grated lemon rind
¼ cup (60ml) lemon juice
⅓ cup (80ml) olive oil

Combine cutlets with spices, rind and oil in large bowl; cover, refrigerate 2 hours or overnight.

Cook cutlets, in batches, in heated oiled griddle pan (or grill or barbecue) until browned both sides and cooked as desired. Serve with Chickpea and Tomato Salad.

Chickpea and Tomato Salad: Mix all ingredients in medium bowl.

Serves 4.

■ Can be prepared a day ahead. Chickpea and Tomato Salad best made just before serving.
■ Storage: Cutlets, covered, in refrigerator.
■ Freeze: Marinated cutlets suitable.
■ Microwave: Not suitable.

OPPOSITE: Beef and Haloumi Kebabs.
ABOVE: Veal Cutlets with Chickpea and Tomato Salad.

MEXICAN BEEF, BEAN AND CORN TOSTADA

Beef strips can be prepared from blade, fillet, rib eye, round, rump, sirloin or topside. We used Old El Paso flour tortillas. To make the foil baskets, cut 6 x 30cm square pieces of foil, shape into baskets with a 12cm base and 4cm sides.

1kg beef strips
1 tablespoon Mexican-style chilli powder
1 tablespoon ground cumin
2 tablespoons chopped fresh oregano leaves
2 cloves garlic, crushed
¼ cup (60ml) tomato paste
¼ cup (60ml) lemon juice
2 small fresh red chillies, seeded, finely chopped
1 medium (200g) red capsicum
2 tablespoons olive oil
1 medium (150g) onion, sliced
310g can corn kernels, drained
300g can kidney beans, rinsed, drained
6 (23cm) flour tortillas
½ cup (125ml) sour cream
¼ cup chopped fresh coriander leaves

Combine beef strips, chilli powder, cumin, oregano, garlic, paste, juice and fresh chillies in medium bowl; cover, refrigerate 3 hours or overnight.

Quarter capsicum, remove seeds and membranes. Roast under grill or in very hot oven, skin side up, until skin blisters and blackens. Cover capsicum pieces in plastic or paper for 5 minutes, peel away skin, slice into strips.

Heat half the oil in large pan; cook undrained marinated beef in batches, stirring, until browned; remove from pan. Heat remaining oil in same pan, add onion, cook until just soft; stir in beef, capsicum, corn and beans, stir until heated through.

Have tortillas at room temperature. Coat both sides with cooking oil spray; gently push into foil baskets. Bake in moderate oven about 15 minutes or until just crisp. Spoon warm beef mixture into tortilla baskets; top with sour cream and coriander.

Serves 6.

- ■ Can be prepared a day ahead.
- ■ Storage: Beef mixture, covered, in refrigerator. Tortilla baskets, in airtight container.
- ■ Freeze: Uncooked marinated strips suitable.
- ■ Microwave: Not suitable.

Plate and glass from Mexico

TARTARE OF BEEF WITH CAPER MAYONNAISE

600g whole piece beef eye fillet, chopped
1 medium (170g) red onion, finely chopped
¼ cup olive oil
¼ cup (30g) finely chopped gherkins
1½ tablespoons capers, chopped
1½ tablespoons Dijon mustard
1 tablespoon Worcestershire sauce
2 tablespoons chopped fresh parsley
½ teaspoon cracked black peppercorns
33cm French bread stick

CAPER MAYONNAISE
2 egg yolks
2 teaspoons Dijon mustard
1 tablespoon lemon juice
¾ cup (180ml) olive oil
3 teaspoons capers, chopped
1 tablespoon water, approximately

Process fillet until finely minced, combine in medium bowl with half the onion (reserve remaining onion for Caper Mayonnaise), half the oil, gherkins, capers, mustard, sauce, parsley and pepper. Cut bread into 2cm diagonal slices, brush with remaining oil; toast or grill until browned both sides. Serve toasted bread with Tartare of Beef and Caper Mayonnaise.

Caper Mayonnaise: Blend or process egg yolks, mustard and juice until smooth. Add oil gradually in a thin stream while motor is operating, blend until mixture thickens. Stir in capers, reserved onion and enough water to give a creamy consistency.

Serves 6 to 8.

■ Best made just before serving.
■ Freeze: Not suitable.
■ Microwave: Not suitable.

TANDOORI BEEF KEBABS

Soak bamboo skewers in water overnight to prevent burning. Beef rib eye roast is also known as whole Scotch fillet.

1kg whole piece beef rib-eye roast
¼ cup (60ml) tandoori paste
¼ cup (60ml) yogurt

CORIANDER SAUCE
¾ cup (180ml) yogurt
⅓ cup firmly packed coriander leaves
1 tablespoon lemon juice
1 clove garlic, peeled, chopped
2 teaspoons sugar

Cut rib eye into 3cm cubes, thread onto 12 skewers. Place kebabs in large shallow dish, pour combined paste and yogurt over. Cover; refrigerate overnight.

Cook kebabs, in batches, in heated oiled griddle pan (or grill or barbecue) until browned all over and cooked as desired. Serve with Coriander Sauce.

Coriander Sauce: Blend or process all ingredients until combined.

Serves 6.

■ Tandoori Beef Kebabs best prepared a day ahead. Coriander Sauce can be made a day ahead.
■ Storage: Rib eye and Sauce, covered, separately, in refrigerator.
■ Freeze: Uncooked marinated Kebabs suitable.
■ Microwave: Not suitable.

BELOW: Tartare of Beef with Caper Mayonnaise.
OPPOSITE: Tandoori Beef Kebabs.

CURRIED BEEF AND VERMICELLI SOUP

Beef rib eye, boneless sirloin and fillet steak are also suitable for this recipe.

2 tablespoons peanut oil
500g rump steak, thinly sliced
1 medium (150g) onion,
   finely chopped
1 clove garlic, crushed
1 small (250g) kumara, chopped
2 tablespoons Madras curry paste
425g can tomatoes
3 cups (750ml) beef stock
50g rice vermicelli noodles,
   chopped
½ cup (125ml) coconut milk
½ cup water
1 tablespoon chopped fresh
   coriander leaves
1 tablespoon chopped fresh
   mint leaves

Heat half the oil in large pan; cook steak, in batches, stirring until browned and almost cooked; remove from pan. Heat remaining oil in same pan, add onion, garlic and kumara; cook, stirring until onion is browned lightly. Add paste; cook, stirring, until fragrant. Add undrained crushed tomatoes and stock; simmer, uncovered, for about 10 minutes or until kumara is almost cooked. Add noodles, simmer, uncovered, about 5 minutes or until noodles and kumara are cooked. Return steak to pan with remaining ingredients; stir until heated through.

Serves 4 to 6.

■ Can be made a day ahead.
■ Storage: Covered, in refrigerator.
■ Freeze: Not suitable.
■ Microwave: Not suitable.

ABOVE: Curried Beef and Vermicelli Soup.
OPPOSITE, TOP: Marinated Ribs.
OPPOSITE, BOTTOM: Gourmet Beef Burgers.

MARINATED RIBS

Order American-style beef spare ribs in advance from the butcher.

2/3 cup (160ml) plum sauce
2/3 cup (160ml) tomato sauce
**1/2 cup (125ml) Worcestershire
 sauce**
2/3 cup (160ml) cider vinegar
**1/2 cup (100g) firmly packed
 brown sugar**
2 small fresh red chillies, chopped
2kg American-style beef spare ribs

Combine sauces, vinegar, sugar and chillies in jug. Cut ribs, between bones, into pieces and place in large shallow dish, pour marinade over. Cover and refrigerate 6 hours or overnight.

Drain ribs over medium bowl; reserve marinade. Place ribs on wire rack over baking dish. Bake, uncovered, in moderate oven about 1 hour or until browned all over and cooked as desired, brushing with the reserved marinade during cooking.

Serves 4.

■ Best prepared a day ahead.
■ Storage: Covered, in refrigerator.
■ Freeze: Uncooked ribs suitable.
■ Microwave: Not suitable.

Tile and plate from Country Floors

GOURMET BEEF BURGERS

750g minced beef
1 cup (70g) stale breadcrumbs
**2 tablespoons chopped
 fresh parsley**
**2 tablespoons sun-dried
 tomato paste**
1 tablespoon olive oil
**125g mozzarella cheese,
 thinly sliced**
1/2 cup (125ml) mayonnaise
4 bread rolls
50g mixed baby lettuce leaves
**1 small (100g) red onion,
 thinly sliced**
**2 tablespoons drained sliced
 sun-dried tomatoes**

Combine mince, breadcrumbs, parsley and 1 1/2 tablespoons of paste in large bowl; shape mixture into 4 patties. Heat oil in pan, add patties; cook until browned both sides and cooked as desired. Place patties on tray; top with mozzarella, grill until melted. Combine remaining paste and mayonnaise in small bowl. Split bread rolls in half, toast cut sides. Sandwich patties, mayonnaise mixture, lettuce, onion and sliced tomatoes between bread rolls.

Serves 4.

■ Patties can be prepared a
 day ahead.
■ Storage: Covered, in refrigerator.
■ Freeze: Uncooked patties suitable.
■ Microwave: Not suitable.

17

VEAL SCALOPPINE

1/4 cup (60ml) olive oil
8 (800g) veal leg schnitzels
1 medium (150g) onion, chopped
2 cloves garlic, crushed
1/3 cup (80ml) lemon juice
1/2 cup (125ml) beef stock
60g butter, chopped
1/3 cup chopped fresh parsley

Heat 2 tablespoons of the oil in large pan; cook schnitzels, in batches, until browned both sides and cooked as desired. Remove from pan; cover to keep warm.

Heat remaining oil in same pan, add onion and garlic; cook, stirring until onion is soft. Stir in lemon juice, stock and butter, simmer, uncovered, about 5 minutes or until mixture thickens slightly; stir in parsley. Serve sauce with Scaloppine.

Serves 4.

■ Best made just before serving.
■ Freeze: Not suitable.
■ Microwave: Not suitable.

BEEF AND NUT BIRYANI

Round steak, skirt steak and gravy beef are also suitable for this recipe. Gravy beef is also known as boneless shin.

750g beef chuck steak
2 teaspoons sambal oelek
2 teaspoons ground coriander
1 teaspoon ground cumin
1 teaspoon ground turmeric
1 tablespoon white vinegar
1/3 cup (80ml) yogurt
2 cups (400g) white long-grain rice
50g ghee
6 cardamom pods
6 whole cloves
2 cinnamon sticks
2 large (400g) onions, chopped
2 1/4 cups (560ml) beef stock
1 cup (125g) frozen peas
3/4 cup (105g) slivered
    almonds, toasted
2 medium (380g) tomatoes,
    chopped
2 tablespoons chopped fresh
    coriander leaves

Cut steak into 3cm cubes, combine with sambal oelek, ground spices, vinegar and yogurt in medium bowl; cover, refrigerate 1 hour. Place rice in bowl, cover with water, stand 30 minutes; drain well.

Melt ghee in large pan, add the cardamom, cloves, cinnamon sticks and onions; cook, stirring, until onions are soft. Add steak; cook, covered, over low heat, stirring occasionally, for about 1 hour or until steak is tender.

Add rice and stock to pan; simmer, covered, about 10 minutes or until rice is just tender, stirring occasionally. Stir in remaining ingredients; cover, stand 5 minutes before serving.

Serves 4 to 6.

■ Can be prepared a day ahead.
■ Storage: Covered, in refrigerator.
■ Freeze: Steak mixture, before the addition of rice and stock, suitable.
■ Microwave: Not suitable.

ABOVE: Beef and Nut Biryani.
OPPOSITE: Veal Scaloppine.

Plates and glass from Villeroy & Boch; bowl, jug, placemat and cushion from Home & Garden on the Mall

MIDDLE EASTERN STEAK SANDWICH

Silverside, rump, round or blade minute steaks are suitable for this recipe.

4 (250g) beef minute steaks
2 medium (300g) onions,
   thinly sliced
3 medium (570g) tomatoes,
   thickly sliced
43cm long Turkish flat bread
8 cos lettuce leaves
1 small (130g) Lebanese
   cucumber, sliced

CORIANDER HUMMUS
½ cup (125ml) hummus
¼ cup (60ml) buttermilk
1 tablespoon chopped fresh
   coriander leaves

Cook steaks, in batches, in heated oiled griddle pan (or grill or barbecue) until browned both sides and cooked as desired. Remove from pan; cover to keep warm.

Add onions and tomatoes to same pan; cook, in batches, until tomatoes are browned and onions soft. Cut bread into 4 pieces; split each piece in half and toast both sides. Sandwich steak, onions and tomatoes, torn lettuce leaves, cucumber and Coriander Hummus between pieces of toast.
Coriander Hummus: Combine all ingredients in small bowl.

Serves 4.

■ Coriander Hummus can be made a day ahead.
■ Storage: Covered, in refrigerator.
■ Freeze: Not suitable.
■ Microwave: Not suitable.

RIB EYE STEAK WITH ROASTED VEGETABLES

Beef rib eye steak is also known as Scotch fillet.

2 medium (400g) red capsicums
2 small (460g) eggplants
2 medium (240g) yellow zucchini
6 (1.3kg) beef rib eye steaks
2 tablespoons olive oil
1 cup (250ml) olive paste

Quarter capsicums, remove seeds and membranes. Roast under grill or in very hot oven, skin side up, until skin blisters and blackens. Cover capsicum pieces in plastic or paper for 5 minutes, peel away skin. Cut eggplants into 2cm slices. Cut zucchini, lengthways, into 2cm slices.

Cook steaks, in batches, in heated oiled griddle pan (or grill or barbecue) until browned both sides and cooked as desired. Cover to keep warm. Heat oil in same pan; cook capsicum, eggplant and zucchini, in batches, until browned all over and soft. Top steaks with capsicum, eggplant, zucchini and olive paste; drizzle with a little extra olive oil, if desired.

Serves 6.

■ Best made just before serving.
■ Freeze: Not suitable.
■ Microwave: Not suitable.

BELOW: Middle Eastern Steak Sandwich.
OPPOSITE: Rib Eye Steak with Roasted Vegetables.

Plate from The Pacific East India Company

SPICY BEEF WITH NOODLES

2 medium (240g) carrots
1kg thick fresh rice noodles
2 tablespoons peanut oil
750g minced beef
1 small (80g) onion, thinly sliced
2 cloves garlic, crushed
1/4 teaspoon Chinese five
    spice powder
1/2 cup (125ml) mild sweet
    chilli sauce
1 bunch (400g) baby bok
    choy, chopped
1/4 cup hoisin sauce
2 tablespoons soy sauce
1 tablespoon fish sauce
2 tablespoons chopped fresh
    coriander leaves

Using a vegetable peeler, cut carrots
into long thin strips.

Place noodles in bowl, cover with
warm water, stand 5 minutes; drain.

Heat oil in wok or large pan, add
mince, onion, garlic and spice; stir-fry
until mince is browned and almost
cooked. Add chilli sauce; stir-fry until
mixture is well browned. Add carrots,
noodles and remaining ingredients;
stir-fry until vegetables are just tender.

Serves 4 to 6.

■ Best made just before serving.
■ Freeze: Not suitable.
■ Microwave: Not suitable.

GINGERED BEEF AND COCONUT SOUP

*Beef rib eye, boneless sirloin and fillet
steak are also suitable for this recipe.
We used South Cape stir-fry noodles
in this recipe; hokkien noodles could
be substituted.*

750g beef rump steak, thinly sliced
1/4 cup red curry paste
1 tablespoon chopped fresh
    lemon grass
1 teaspoon grated lime rind
1/3 cup (80ml) lime juice
500g stir-fry noodles
1 tablespoon peanut oil
1 tablespoon grated fresh ginger
1 litre (4 cups) beef stock
2 x 400ml cans coconut milk
6 kaffir lime leaves
1 tablespoon brown sugar
1 tablespoon fish sauce
425g can straw mushrooms,
    drained, halved
1/4 cup chopped fresh
    coriander leaves
1/4 cup lightly packed fresh
    mint leaves
100g watercress

Combine steak, 1 tablespoon of the
curry paste, lemon grass, rind and 1
tablespoon of the juice in bowl; cover,
refrigerate 3 hours or overnight.

Place noodles in large bowl, cover with
boiling water, stand 5 minutes; drain.

Heat oil in large pan; cook steak, in
batches, until browned and almost
cooked; remove from pan. Add remaining curry paste and ginger to same
pan; cook, stirring, over low heat until
fragrant. Add remaining juice, stock,
coconut milk, lime leaves, sugar and
sauce; simmer, covered, 30 minutes.
Strain soup; discard lime leaves.
Combine strained soup, noodles,
steak, mushrooms and coriander in
same pan; simmer, uncovered, until
heated through. Serve hot soup sprinkled with mint and watercress.

Serves 4 to 6.

■ Steak can be prepared a day ahead.
■ Storage: Covered, in refrigerator.
■ Freeze: Not suitable.
■ Microwave: Not suitable.

*OPPOSITE: Spicy Beef with Noodles.
ABOVE: Gingered Beef and Coconut Soup.*

Plate from Villeroy & Boch

STEAK DIANE

Beef rib eye, boneless sirloin and rump steak are also suitable for this recipe.

1½ tablespoons vegetable oil
4 (about 800g) beef eye fillet steaks
30g butter
2 cloves garlic, crushed
1¼ cups (300ml) thickened cream
**2 tablespoons Worcestershire
   sauce**
1 tablespoon brandy
**¼ teaspoon cracked black
   peppercorns**

Heat oil in large pan, add steaks; cook until browned both sides and cooked as desired. Remove from pan; cover to keep warm. Melt butter in same pan, add garlic; cook, stirring, until soft. Stir in cream, sauce, brandy and peppercorns; simmer, stirring, about 2 minutes or until sauce thickens slightly. Return steaks and any juices to pan, coat with sauce; serve immediately.

Serves 4.

■ Must be made just before serving.
■ Freeze: Not suitable.
■ Microwave: Not suitable.

BEEF FRIED RICE

You will need to cook about 1 cup long-grain rice for this recipe. Beef strips can be prepared from blade, fillet, rib eye, round, rump, sirloin or topside.

3 cups cooked long-grain rice
2 tablespoons peanut oil
2 eggs, lightly beaten
500g medium uncooked prawns
500g beef strips
1 teaspoon sesame oil
1 medium (150g) onion, sliced
2 cloves garlic, crushed
**2 teaspoons finely grated
   fresh ginger**
1 medium (120g) carrot, sliced
1 cup (125g) frozen peas
130g can corn kernels, drained
4 green onions, sliced
1½ tablespoons soy sauce

Spread rice over shallow tray; refrigerate, uncovered, overnight.

Heat 1 teaspoon of the peanut oil in wok or large pan, add half the eggs, swirl wok so eggs form a thin omelette; cook until set. Transfer omelette to board, roll tightly, cut into thin strips. Repeat with 1 teaspoon of the oil and

remaining eggs. Shell and devein prawns, leaving tails intact.

Heat half the remaining peanut oil in wok or large pan; stir-fry beef strips, in batches, until browned and just cooked; remove from wok.

Heat remaining peanut oil and sesame oil in wok, add onion, garlic, ginger and carrot; stir-fry until the vegetables are just tender. Add prawns, stir-fry until just cooked.

Add rice, omelette, beef, peas, corn, green onions and sauce, stir-fry until heated through.

Serves 4 to 6.

■ Rice best cooked a day ahead.
■ Storage: Uncovered, in refrigerator.
■ Freeze: Cooked rice suitable.
■ Microwave: Rice suitable.

ABOVE: Steak Diane.
OPPOSITE: Beef Fried Rice.

Bowls from The Bay Tree Kitchen Shop

Bowl from Bondi Storehouse

SWEET AND SOUR BEEF

Beef strips can be prepared from blade, fillet, rib eye, round, rump, sirloin or topside.

2 tablespoons peanut oil
750g beef strips
2 cloves garlic, crushed
2 teaspoons finely grated fresh ginger
1 medium (150g) onion, sliced
1 medium (120g) carrot, sliced
200g button mushrooms, sliced
1 small (150g) red capsicum, sliced
1 small (150g) green capsicum, sliced
3/4 cup (180ml) pineapple juice
1/4 cup (60ml) tomato sauce
1 tablespoon cornflour
2 tablespoons brown malt vinegar
1 tablespoon brown sugar
1/2 small (400g) pineapple, quartered, sliced
2 tablespoons chopped fresh coriander leaves

Heat half the oil in wok or large pan; stir-fry beef strips, in batches, until browned and almost cooked; remove from wok. Heat remaining oil in wok, add garlic, ginger and onion; stir-fry until onion is soft. Add carrot, mushrooms and capsicums; stir-fry until vegetables are just tender.

Return beef to wok with juice, sauce and blended cornflour, vinegar and sugar; stir until mixture boils and thickens. Add pineapple and coriander, stir until heated through.

Serves 4 to 6.

▇ Best made just before serving.
▇ Freeze: Not suitable.
▇ Microwave: Not suitable.

Plate from Villeroy & Boch

BEEF AND REEF

Beef rib eye, boneless sirloin and rump steak are also suitable for this recipe.

18 (650g) medium uncooked king prawns
2 cups (500ml) water
1/2 cup (125ml) dry white wine
2 bay leaves
6 black peppercorns
1 small (70g) carrot, chopped
2 small (160g) onions, chopped
6 (1.1kg) beef eye fillet steaks
2 tablespoons olive oil
20g butter
1/2 cup (125ml) cream

Shell and devein prawns, leaving tails intact; reserve the shells. Combine reserved prawn shells, water, wine, bay leaves, peppercorns, carrot and half the onion in medium pan; simmer, uncovered about 5 minutes or until mixture has reduced by about one-third. Strain mixture over medium bowl; reserve stock.

Tie steaks into rounds with string to hold shape. Heat oil and butter in same pan; cook steaks, in batches, until browned both sides and cooked as desired. Remove from pan, discard string, cover to keep warm.

Add prawns to same pan; stir over heat until just cooked. Remove from pan, cover to keep warm. Add remaining onion to same pan; cook, stirring, until onion is soft. Add reserved stock and cream, simmer, uncovered, about 5 minutes or until mixture has reduced by about one-third. Serve sauce over steaks topped with prawns.

Serves 6.
- Best made just before serving.
- Storage: Covered, in refrigerator.
- Freeze: Prawn stock suitable.
- Microwave: Not suitable.

CAJUN BLACKENED STEAK WITH TABASCO BUTTER

Boneless sirloin steak is also known as New York cut.

1/3 cup (40g) hot paprika
1/3 cup (50g) cracked black peppercorns
2 teaspoons cayenne pepper
3 cloves garlic, crushed
1/3 cup chopped fresh thyme leaves
6 (1.3kg) boneless beef sirloin steaks
125g butter, melted
1 teaspoon Tabasco sauce

Combine paprika, peppers, garlic and thyme in small bowl. Brush steaks both sides with some of the butter; coat with pepper mixture. Cook steaks in heated oiled griddle pan until browned both sides and cooked as desired. Remove from griddle pan; cover to keep warm. Combine remaining butter and sauce in small pan; heat until bubbling, serve over steaks.

Serves 6.
- Best made just before serving.
- Freeze: Not suitable.
- Microwave: Not suitable.

OPPOSITE TOP: Sweet and Sour Beef.
OPPOSITE BOTTOM: Beef and Reef.
ABOVE: Cajun Blackened Steak with Tabasco Sauce.

PEPPERY GARLIC RIB STEAKS

6 (1.8kg) beef rib steaks
1/4 cup chopped fresh
    oregano leaves
2 small fresh red chillies, chopped
2 cloves garlic, crushed
1/3 cup (80ml) lemon juice
1/4 cup (60ml) olive oil
2 teaspoons cracked black
    peppercorns
6 small (360g) parsnips, peeled
250g shallots, peeled
2 tablespoons brown sugar

Combine steaks, oregano, chillies, garlic, juice, oil and peppercorns in large shallow dish; cover, refrigerate 6 hours or overnight.

Drain steaks over medium bowl; reserve marinade. Cook steaks, in batches, in heated oiled griddle pan (or grill or barbecue) until browned both sides and cooked as desired. Boil, steam or microwave parsnips and shallots until just tender; drain. Place reserved marinade in medium pan; bring to boil. Add sugar, stir over heat, without boiling, until sugar is dissolved. Add parsnips and shallots; stir gently to coat vegetables. Serve with steaks.

Serves 4 to 6.

■ Best made just before serving.
■ Freeze: Marinated steaks suitable.
■ Microwave: Vegetables suitable.

VEAL SOUVLAKIA WITH TOMATO AND ONION SALSA

*Soak bamboo skewers in water
overnight to prevent burning.*

1kg whole piece veal fillets
4 medium pitta bread rounds

MARINADE
1 small (80g) onion,
    roughly chopped
2 cloves garlic, peeled, chopped
1/4 cup (60ml) yogurt
1 tablespoon lemon juice
1 tablespoon olive oil
1/4 cup firmly packed mint leaves
3 teaspoons white wine vinegar

TOMATO AND ONION SALSA
4 medium (300g) egg tomatoes,
    seeded, chopped
1 medium (150g) onion, chopped
2 tablespoons chopped fresh
    mint leaves
1 teaspoon ground sweet paprika

YOGURT SAUCE
3/4 cup (180ml) yogurt
2 teaspoons tahini
1 tablespoon hot water

Cut fillets into 3cm cubes, thread onto 10 skewers. Combine skewers and marinade in large shallow dish; cover, refrigerate 3 hours or overnight. Cook skewers, in batches, in heated oiled griddle pan (or grill or barbecue) until browned all over and cooked as desired. Serve with Tomato and Onion Salsa, Yogurt Sauce and warm pitta bread.

Marinade: Process all ingredients until combined.

Tomato and Onion Salsa: Combine all ingredients in small bowl.

Yogurt Sauce: Whisk all the ingredients in small bowl until combined.

Serves 4 to 6.

■ Fillets best prepared a day ahead. Tomato and Onion Salsa and Yogurt Sauce can be made a day ahead.
■ Storage: Covered, separately, in refrigerator.
■ Freeze: Not suitable.
■ Microwave: Not suitable.

*BELOW: Peppery Garlic Rib Steaks.
OPPOSITE: Veal Souvlakia with Tomato and Onion Salsa.*

Tray from Accoutrement

Tray and pepper mill from Ventura Design; plate from Wednesdays Value Homewares

HONEY-GARLIC BEEF STIR-FRY

Beef strips can be prepared from blade, fillet, rib eye, round, rump, sirloin or topside.

1kg beef strips
4 cloves garlic, crushed
1/2 teaspoon five-spice powder
1 tablespoon grated fresh ginger
1 tablespoon sweet sherry
1/4 cup (60ml) honey
1 tablespoon thick soy sauce
2 tablespoons peanut oil
**1 medium (200g) red capsicum,
thinly sliced**
**1 medium (200g) green capsicum,
thinly sliced**
**1 medium (200g) yellow capsicum,
thinly sliced**

Combine beef strips, garlic, five-spice, ginger, sherry, honey and sauce in medium bowl; cover, refrigerate for 3 hours or overnight.

Drain beef over medium bowl; reserve marinade. Heat half the oil in wok or large pan; stir-fry beef, in batches, until browned and just cooked; remove from wok. Heat remaining oil in same wok, add capsicums and reserved marinade; stir-fry until capsicums are just tender; add beef, stir-fry until heated through.

Serves 6.

■ Can be prepared a day ahead.
■ Storage: Covered, in refrigerator.
■ Freeze: Uncooked marinated beef suitable.
■ Microwave: Not suitable.

MEDITERRANEAN STEAK TOWERS

Beef rump, boneless sirloin and rib eye steaks are also suitable for this recipe.

1 large (350g) red capsicum
1 large (500g) eggplant, sliced
**2 medium (240g) zucchini,
thinly sliced**
2 tablespoons olive oil
4 (900g) beef fillet steaks
40cm long Turkish flat bread
30g mixed baby lettuce leaves

BALSAMIC DRESSING
1/3 cup (80ml) olive oil
2 tablespoons balsamic vinegar

Quarter capsicum, remove seeds and membranes. Roast under grill or in very hot oven, skin side up, until skin blisters

and blackens. Cover capsicum pieces in plastic or paper for 5 minutes, peel away skin, slice into thin strips; cover to keep warm. Brush eggplant and zucchini with oil; cook, in batches, in heated oiled griddle pan (or grill or barbecue) until browned and tender; cover to keep warm.

Pound each steak with a meat mallet until an even thickness. Cook steaks in heated oiled griddle pan until browned both sides and cooked as desired. Meanwhile, cut bread into 4 pieces; toast bread. Top toast with lettuce leaves, eggplant, steak, capsicum and zucchini. Drizzle with Balsamic Dressing.

Balsamic Dressing: Combine oil and vinegar in jar; shake well.

Serves 4.

■ Capsicum, eggplant and zucchini can be cooked up to 2 hours ahead.
■ Storage: Covered, separately, in refrigerator.
■ Freeze: Not suitable.
■ Microwave: Not suitable.

VEAL CUTLETS WITH ROASTED TOMATO SALAD

6 (750g) veal cutlets
6 small (360g) egg tomatoes, halved
¼ cup fresh basil leaves
1 cup (80g) mung bean sprouts
4 green onions, chopped
¼ cup (35g) drained sun-dried tomatoes, sliced

GARLIC DRESSING
½ cup (125ml) olive oil
2 tablespoons balsamic vinegar
2 cloves garlic, crushed
1 teaspoon English mustard

Cook cutlets, in batches, in heated oiled griddle pan (or grill or barbecue) until browned both sides and cooked as desired. Remove from pan; cover to keep warm. Add egg tomatoes, cut side down, to same pan; cook until browned and soft. Combine egg tomatoes, basil, sprouts, onions, sun-dried tomatoes and Garlic Dressing in medium bowl; serve over cutlets.

Garlic Dressing: Combine all ingredients in jar; shake well.

Serves 4 to 6.

■ Best made just before serving. Garlic Dressing can be made a day ahead.
■ Storage: Covered, in refrigerator.
■ Freeze: Not suitable.
■ Microwave: Not suitable.

OPPOSITE: Honey-Garlic Beef Stir-Fry.
ABOVE RIGHT: Mediterranean Steak Towers.
RIGHT: Veal Cutlets with Roasted Tomato Salad.

TRIPLE-CHEESE CRUMBED BEEF STEAKS

We used beef fillet from the rump in this recipe. This is also known as butt fillet.

750g whole piece beef fillet
plain flour
1 egg
¼ cup (60ml) milk
½ cup (60g) finely grated tasty cheddar cheese
½ cup (40g) finely grated parmesan cheese
½ cup (40g) finely grated romano cheese
1 cup (70g) stale breadcrumbs
1 tablespoon olive oil

MUSTARD BUTTER SAUCE
1 tablespoon seeded mustard
¼ cup (60ml) chicken stock
60g butter, chopped
1 tablespoon chopped fresh chives

Cut fillet into 1.5cm steaks. Toss steaks in flour; shake off excess. Dip in combined egg and milk; coat with combined cheeses and breadcrumbs. Place steaks on tray, cover, refrigerate 30 minutes.

Heat oil in pan; cook steaks, in batches, until browned both sides and cooked as desired. Serve with Mustard Butter Sauce.

Mustard Butter Sauce: Combine the mustard and stock in pan; stir over heat until hot. Remove from heat, whisk in butter, in batches; whisk until smooth; stir in chives.

Serves 4 to 6.
- Steaks can be prepared 3 hours ahead.
- Storage: Covered, in refrigerator.
- Freeze: Not suitable.
- Microwave: Not suitable.

MONGOLIAN-STYLE BEEF STIR-FRY

Beef strips can be prepared from blade, fillet, rib eye, round, rump, sirloin or topside.

2 tablespoons peanut oil
750g beef strips
2 cloves garlic, crushed
2 teaspoons finely grated fresh ginger
2 large (400g) onions, sliced
1 teaspoon sesame oil
2 tablespoons salt-reduced soy sauce
¼ cup (60ml) hoisin sauce
2 teaspoons cornflour
½ cup (125ml) beef stock
2 teaspoons sesame seeds, toasted

Heat half the peanut oil in wok or large pan; stir-fry beef strips, in batches, until browned and almost cooked; remove from wok.

Heat remaining peanut oil in same wok, add garlic, ginger and onions; stir-fry until onions are soft. Return beef to wok with sesame oil, sauces and the blended cornflour and stock, stir until mixture boils and thickens. Serve sprinkled with sesame seeds.

Serves 4 to 6.
- Best made just before serving.
- Freeze: Not suitable.
- Microwave: Not suitable.

OPPOSITE: Triple-Cheese Crumbed Beef Steaks.
BELOW: Mongolian-Style Beef Stir-Fry.

VEAL SCHNITZEL

12 (1.2kg) veal leg schnitzels
plain flour
3 eggs, lightly beaten
3 cups (210g) stale breadcrumbs
2/3 cup chopped fresh basil leaves
1/3 cup (80ml) olive oil

TOMATO SAUCE
1 tablespoon olive oil
2 medium (300g) onions, chopped
3 cloves garlic, crushed
6 medium (1kg) tomatoes, chopped
2 tablespoons balsamic vinegar
2 tablespoons brown sugar

Place schnitzels between sheets of plastic wrap; pound gently with meat mallet until an even thickness. Toss schnitzels in flour; shake off excess. Dip in eggs, then coat in combined breadcrumbs and basil. Heat oil in large pan; cook schnitzels, in batches, until browned both sides and cooked as desired. Serve with Tomato Sauce.
Tomato Sauce: Heat oil in medium pan, add the onions and garlic; cook, stirring, until onions are soft. Add the remaining ingredients, simmer, uncovered, about 10 minutes or until tomatoes are pulpy. Blend or process mixture until combined.

Serves 6 to 8.

■ Schnitzels can be prepared a day ahead. Tomato Sauce can be made 3 days ahead.
■ Storage: Covered, separately, in refrigerator.
■ Freeze: Crumbed, uncooked schnitzels suitable.
■ Microwave: Sauce suitable.

Plate from Grace Bros

Lazy Susan from Mosmania; oil container from Home & Garden on the Mall

KASHMIRI MEATBALLS WITH SPINACH RAITA

Soak bamboo skewers in water overnight to prevent burning.

2 teaspoons vegetable oil
1 medium (150g) onion,
finely chopped
2 cloves garlic, crushed
2 teaspoons grated fresh ginger
1/4 cup (60ml) Madras curry paste
1/4 cup chopped fresh
coriander leaves
1/3 cup (55g) finely chopped raisins
1/4 cup (35g) cashews, toasted,
finely chopped
850g minced beef

SPINACH RAITA
1 bunch (500g) English spinach
3/4 cup (180ml) yogurt
1 teaspoon lemon juice
1/2 teaspoon ground cumin
1/2 teaspoon sugar

Heat oil in medium pan, add onion, garlic, ginger and paste; cook, stirring, until onion is soft. Combine onion mixture with remaining ingredients in large bowl, mix well; cover, refrigerate 1 hour.

Roll level tablespoons of mixture into balls; thread balls onto 12 skewers. Cook skewers, in batches, in heated oiled griddle pan (or grill or barbecue) until browned all over and cooked as desired. Serve with Spinach Raita.

Spinach Raita: Boil, steam or microwave spinach leaves until just wilted; drain, squeeze out excess liquid. Blend or process spinach with remaining ingredients until smooth.

Serves 4.

■ Kashmiri Meatballs can be prepared a day ahead. Spinach Raita best made just before serving.
■ Storage: Meatballs and Raita, covered, separately, in refrigerator.
■ Freeze: Meatballs suitable.
■ Microwave: Spinach suitable.

MULLIGATAWNY SOUP

We used beef fillet from the rump in this recipe. This is also known as butt fillet.

1 tablespoon vegetable oil
2 medium (300g) onions, chopped
3 cloves garlic, crushed
2 teaspoons grated fresh ginger
1/4 cup (60ml) mild curry paste
8 fresh curry leaves
1 cup (200g) red lentils
2 medium (400g) potatoes, chopped
1 large (200g) apple,
    peeled, chopped
1.5 litres (6 cups) beef stock
1 cinnamon stick
2 teaspoons vegetable oil, extra
400g whole piece beef fillet,
    thinly sliced
1 cup (250ml) coconut milk
2 tablespoons lemon juice
2 tablespoons chopped fresh
    coriander leaves

Heat oil in large pan, add onions, garlic, ginger, paste and curry leaves; cook, stirring, until onions are soft. Rinse lentils under cold water, add to same pan with potatoes, apple, stock and the cinnamon stick; simmer, covered, about 20 minutes or until potatoes are soft.

Remove and reserve curry leaves; discard cinnamon stick. Blend or process lentil mixture until smooth; return to pan. Heat extra oil in large pan; cook fillet, in batches, stirring until browned and almost cooked. Chop fillet roughly, add to lentil mixture with reserved curry leaves, coconut milk, juice and coriander; stir until heated through.

Serves 6.

■ Can be made a day ahead.
■ Storage: Covered, in refrigerator.
■ Freeze: Not suitable.
■ Microwave: Not suitable.

OPPOSITE BOTTOM: Veal Schnitzel.
OPPOSITE TOP: Kashmiri Meatballs with Spinach Raita.
ABOVE: Mulligatawny Soup.

OLIVE AND CHILLI CHEESEBURGERS

500g minced beef
1 medium (170g) red onion,
**   finely chopped**
¼ cup (40g) seeded black
**   olives, chopped**
1 tablespoon chopped capers
2 tablespoons chopped fresh
**   basil leaves**
1 tablespoon tomato paste
1 clove garlic, crushed
1 small fresh red chilli,
**   seeded, chopped**
1 egg, lightly beaten
⅔ cup (50g) stale breadcrumbs
2 large (700g) red capsicums
vegetable oil, for shallow-frying
8 bread rolls
8 (160g) cheese slices
1 large (320g) avocado, sliced
⅓ cup (80ml) sweet chilli sauce

Combine mince, onion, olives, capers, basil, paste, garlic, chilli, egg and breadcrumbs in bowl; cover, refrigerate 30 minutes.

Shape mixture into 8 patties. Quarter capsicums, remove seeds and membranes. Roast under grill or in very hot oven, skin side up, until skin blisters and blackens. Cover capsicum pieces in plastic or paper for 5 minutes, peel away skin, slice thickly.

Shallow-fry patties in hot oil until browned both sides and cooked as desired; drain on absorbent paper. Split rolls in half; toast cut sides. Place patties on bases of rolls; top with cheese slices, grill until melted. Top with roasted capsicum and avocado; drizzle with sweet chilli sauce.

Serves 4.

■ Can be prepared a day ahead.
■ Storage: Covered, in refrigerator.
■ Freeze: Uncooked patties suitable.
■ Microwave: Not suitable.

HOT AND SOUR SOUP WITH BEEF DUMPLINGS

1 tablespoon peanut oil
1 tablespoon chopped fresh
**   lemon grass**
4 cloves garlic, crushed
1 tablespoon grated fresh ginger
3 small fresh red chillies, chopped
2 tablespoons tamarind pulp
**   concentrate**
2 tablespoons fish sauce
2 litres (8 cups) beef stock
¼ cup chopped fresh mint leaves
¼ cup chopped fresh
**   coriander leaves**
2 teaspoons sugar
6 green onions, chopped
1 cup (80g) mung bean sprouts

BEEF DUMPLINGS
6 dried Chinese mushrooms
1 tablespoon chopped fresh
**   coriander leaves**
500g minced beef
½ cup (35g) stale breadcrumbs
1 egg yolk
2 tablespoons peanut oil

Heat oil in medium pan, add lemon grass, garlic, ginger and chillies; cook, stirring until lemon grass is soft. Add remaining ingredients, bring to boil; add beef dumplings, stir until heated through.
Beef Dumplings: Place mushrooms in small bowl, cover with boiling water, stand 20 minutes; drain. Discard stalks, chop caps. Combine the mushrooms, coriander, mince, breadcrumbs and egg yolk in medium bowl, mix well; shape level tablespoons of mixture into balls. Heat oil in pan; cook dumplings, in batches, until browned all over; drain on absorbent paper.

Serves 4.

■ Beef Dumplings can be made
    a day ahead. Soup best made
    just before serving.
■ Storage: Beef dumplings, covered,
    in refrigerator.
■ Freeze: Not suitable.
■ Microwave: Not suitable.

*OPPOSITE: Olive and Chilli
Cheeseburgers.
BELOW: Hot and Sour Soup
with Beef Dumplings.*

HONEY MUSTARD BEEF RIBS

*Order American-style beef spare ribs
in advance from the butcher.*

1/2 cup (125ml) honey
1/2 cup (125ml) green ginger wine
2 tablespoons seeded mustard
2 cloves garlic, crushed
**1.5kg (about 2) American-style
   beef spare ribs**

Combine honey, wine, mustard and
garlic in jug. Place ribs in large flat dish.
Pour marinade over ribs, cover; refrigerate 3 hours or overnight, turning ribs
occasionally.

Drain ribs over medium bowl;
reserve marinade. Place ribs on wire
rack over oven tray. Bake, uncovered,
in moderate oven about 1 1/2 hours or
until browned all over and cooked as
desired, brushing occasionally with
reserved marinade.

Serves 4 to 6.
- Best prepared a day ahead.
- Storage: Covered, in refrigerator.
- Freeze: Uncooked marinated
  ribs suitable.
- Microwave: Not suitable.

VEAL PASTA SALAD WITH LIME MUSTARD DRESSING

250g tagliatelle pasta
750g veal rump steak
200g fetta cheese, chopped
**1/2 cup (75g) drained sun-dried
   tomatoes, sliced**
1/4 cup (40g) pine nuts, toasted
100g mixed baby lettuce leaves
1/2 cup (60g) seeded black olives

LIME MUSTARD DRESSING
1/3 cup (80ml) olive oil
3 teaspoons seeded mustard
1 teaspoon sugar
2 tablespoons lime juice

Cook pasta in large pan of boiling water
until just tender; drain. Rinse under
cold water; drain.

Cook steak in heated oiled griddle
pan (or grill or barbecue) until browned
both sides and cooked as desired.
Remove steak from pan, cover; stand
for 5 minutes. Slice steak thinly.
Combine all ingredients in large bowl
with Lime Mustard Dressing.
Lime Mustard Dressing: Combine all
ingredients in jar; shake well.

Serves 4 to 6.
- Best made on day of serving.
- Storage: Covered, in refrigerator.
- Freeze: Not suitable.
- Microwave: Pasta suitable.

ABOVE: Honey Mustard Beef Ribs.
*OPPOSITE: Veal Pasta Salad with
Lime Mustard Dressing.*

CRISP SHREDDED BEEF WITH CHOY SUM

750g whole piece beef eye fillet
1/3 cup (80ml) Chinese barbecue
**   sauce**
1/3 cup (80ml) hoisin sauce
1 teaspoon chilli oil
2 tablespoons cornflour
2 bunches (1.2kg) choy sum,
**   shredded**
vegetable oil, for deep-frying
plain flour

Cut fillet into 5mm strips, combine in medium bowl with sauces, chilli oil and cornflour; cover, refrigerate for 3 hours or overnight.

Deep-fry choy sum, in batches, in hot oil until crisp; drain in single layer on absorbent paper. Toss beef strips in flour; shake off excess. Deep-fry beef, in batches, in hot oil until browned and crisp; drain on absorbent paper. Serve beef with choy sum.

Serves 4.
- Best made just before serving.
- Freeze: Not suitable.
- Microwave: Not suitable.

BEEF AND VEGETABLE SOUP

Beef rib eye, boneless sirloin and fillet steak are also suitable for this recipe.

500g beef rump steak
1 tablespoon olive oil
1 large (200g) onion, finely chopped
2 cloves garlic, crushed
3 (200g) bacon rashers,
**   finely chopped**
2 medium (240g) carrots,
**   finely chopped**
1 small (250g) kumara,
**   finely chopped**
2 medium (400g) potatoes,
**   finely chopped**
1.5 litres (6 cups) water
2 teaspoons beef stock powder
425g can tomatoes
8 English spinach leaves,
**   finely shredded**
2 teaspoons chopped fresh
**   thyme leaves**

Cook steak in oiled greased griddle pan (or grill or barbecue) until browned both sides and cooked as desired. Cool steak; slice thinly.

Heat oil in large pan, add the onion, garlic and bacon; cook, stirring, until onion is soft. Add carrots, kumara, potatoes, water, stock powder and undrained crushed tomatoes; simmer, uncovered, about 30 minutes or until vegetables are tender. Add steak, spinach and thyme; stir until heated through.

Serves 6.
- Can be made a day ahead.
- Storage: Covered, in refrigerator.
- Freeze: Suitable.
- Microwave: Not suitable.

OPPOSITE: Crisp Shredded Beef with Choy Sum.
BELOW: Beef and Vegetable Soup.

SUKIYAKI

A traditional Sukiyaki pan can be purchased from stores which stock Japanese or Asian goods, however, an electric fry pan is a good substitute. Small quantities of Sukiyaki are cooked and served individually to guests at the table. Each guest usually has a small bowl containing a raw egg which has been lightly beaten with chopsticks; the hot food is dipped into the egg before being eaten. Always serve Sukiyaki with rice. Partially freeze beef to make slicing easier.

750g whole piece beef eye fillet
300g Chinese cabbage, chopped
8 green onions, chopped
200g oyster mushrooms
200g mung bean sprouts
100g snow peas
100g bean thread noodles
110g pickled ginger

MIRIN SAUCE
1¼ cups (310ml) mirin
½ cup (125ml) light salt-reduced soy sauce
2 teaspoons sugar
1 teaspoon instant dashi powder
2 cups (500ml) water

Slice fillet thinly, arrange with remaining ingredients on plate. Cook a selection of ingredients, in batches, in simmering Mirin Sauce; serve immediately.
Mirin Sauce: Combine all ingredients in pan; stir over heat until simmering.
Serves 4 to 6.

■ Best made just before serving.
■ Freeze: Not suitable.
■ Microwave: Not suitable

ASIAN-STYLE CHILLI BEEF SKEWERS

Soak bamboo skewers in water overnight to prevent burning.

1kg beef rump steaks
¼ cup (60ml) mild sweet chilli sauce
⅓ cup (80ml) plum sauce
⅓ cup (80ml) soy sauce
1 teaspoon sesame oil
4 cloves garlic, crushed
1 tablespoon grated fresh ginger
¼ cup chopped fresh coriander leaves

Cut steaks into 3mm slices across the grain. Combine steak slices with remaining ingredients in medium bowl; cover, refrigerate 3 hours or overnight.
Thread steak onto 25 skewers. Cook skewers, in batches, in heated oiled griddle pan (or grill or barbecue) until browned all over and cooked as desired.
Serves 6.

■ Best prepared a day ahead.
■ Storage: Covered, in refrigerator.
■ Freeze: Uncooked skewers suitable.
■ Microwave: Not suitable.

SMOKED BEEF

This recipe can be made in a wok or a kettle-style barbecue. We used Weber Hickory Wood Chunks but any hardwood chips packaged for home barbecuing can be substituted.

350g wood-smoking chips
½ cup (125ml) dry red wine
1 tablespoon olive oil
750g whole piece beef eye fillet
12 cloves unpeeled garlic

Place chips and red wine in medium bowl, stand 30 minutes. Heat oil in large pan, add beef fillet; cook until well browned all over.

To smoke in wok: Line wok or a large pan with foil; place drained chips on foil then wire rack over chips. Place fillet and garlic on rack, cover wok tightly with foil. Cook over medium heat about 25 minutes or until fillet is cooked as desired. Cover fillet, stand 5 minutes before serving with garlic.

To smoke in kettle-style barbecue: Use indirect method of cooking. When coals are ready, place the disposable aluminium drip tray filled with 3 cups water on centre grate; place drained chips on top of coals. Replace top the barbecue grill, cover with lid briefly, until fragrant smoke develops. Lift lid, place

fillet and garlic onto barbecue grill; cover, smoke about 30 minutes or until fillet is cooked as desired. Cover fillet, stand for 5 minutes before serving with garlic.

Serves 6 to 8.

- Can be prepared a day ahead.
- Storage: Covered, in refrigerator.
- Freeze: Not suitable.
- Microwave: Not suitable.

OPPOSITE, TOP: Sukiyaki.
OPPOSITE, BOTTOM: Asian-Style Chilli Beef Skewers.
ABOVE: Smoked Beef.

43

Decorative eggplant from Sirocco Homewares; cutlery from Kitchen Kapers

Tiles from Bisanna Tiles

VEAL PARMIGIANO

1 medium (300g) eggplant
8 (800g) veal leg steaks
plain flour
2 tablespoons olive oil
1 clove garlic, crushed
4 large (1kg) tomatoes, chopped
¼ cup shredded fresh basil leaves
1 teaspoon sugar
1 cup (100g) grated
   mozzarella cheese
1 tablespoon grated
   Parmesan cheese

Cut eggplant lengthways into 8 slices, make shallow cuts in criss cross pattern on one side of each slice. Coat both sides with cooking oil spray; grill until browned and softened. Place steaks between sheets of plastic wrap; pound gently with meat mallet until an even thickness. Toss in flour; shake off excess. Heat half the oil in large pan; cook steaks, in batches, until browned both sides and cooked as desired. Remove from pan; cover to keep warm.

Heat remaining oil in same pan, add garlic; cook until soft. Add tomatoes, basil and sugar, simmer, uncovered, about 15 minutes or until tomatoes are soft and sauce thickens.

Top each steak with slice of eggplant, spoon sauce over; sprinkle with cheeses. Grill steaks until cheeses have melted.

Serves 4 to 6.

■ Can be prepared 3 hours ahead.
■ Storage: Covered, in refrigerator.
■ Freeze: Not suitable.
■ Microwave: Not suitable.

THAI-STYLE SWEET CHILLI RIBS

Order beef short ribs in advance from the butcher.

1.5kg (4 pieces) beef short ribs
½ cup (125ml) mild sweet
   chilli sauce
2 tablespoons fish sauce
2 tablespoons rice wine
2 cloves garlic, crushed
1 tablespoon chopped fresh
   coriander leaves

Cut ribs in half. Combine ribs in large bowl with remaining ingredients; cover, refrigerate 3 hours or overnight.

Drain ribs over bowl; reserve the marinade. Place ribs on wire rack, grill until cooked as desired, brushing with reserved marinade during cooking. Place remaining marinade in small pan; bring to boil; serve with ribs.

Serves 4.

■ Can be marinated 2 days ahead.
■ Storage: Covered, in refrigerator.
■ Freeze: Not suitable.
■ Microwave: Not suitable.

LEFT: Veal Parmigiano.
OPPOSITE: Thai-Style Sweet Chilli Ribs.

THE GREAT BEEF COOKBOOK

SPICY KEBABS WITH FRUITY COUSCOUS

Soak bamboo skewers in water overnight to prevent burning. Beef rib eye roast is also known as whole Scotch fillet.

750g whole piece beef rib eye roast
2 teaspoons ground cumin
2 teaspoons ground coriander
½ teaspoon chilli powder
1 cup (250ml) yogurt
¼ cup (60ml) buttermilk
2 tablespoons water
1 clove garlic, crushed
1 tablespoon chopped fresh mint leaves

FRUITY COUSCOUS
2 tablespoons olive oil
2 small (160g) onions, thinly sliced
1 teaspoon ground cumin
½ cup (75g) dried apricots, thinly sliced
⅓ cup (50g) dried currants
3 teaspoons chicken stock powder
1½ cups (300g) couscous
1½ cups (375ml) boiling water

Cut rib eye into 3cm cubes, thread onto 8 skewers. Coat kebabs with combined spices. Cook kebabs, in batches, in heated oiled griddle pan (or grill or barbecue) until browned all over and cooked as desired. Serve Spicy Kebabs with Fruity Couscous; drizzle with combined remaining ingredients.

Fruity Couscous: Heat oil in medium pan, add onions; cook, stirring, until soft. Add cumin; cook, stirring until fragrant; stir in remaining ingredients. Remove from heat, stand, covered, for 5 minutes or until water is absorbed.

Serves 4 to 6.

▓ Spicy Kebabs can be prepared a day ahead. Yogurt mixture can be made a day ahead.

▓ Storage: Covered, separately, in refrigerator.

▓ Freeze: Uncooked Kebabs suitable.

▓ Microwave: Fruity Couscous suitable.

Colander and pepper grinder from House In Newtown

CARPETBAG STEAK

Beef rib eye, boneless sirloin or rump steak are also suitable for this recipe.

12 oysters
1 tablespoon lemon juice
1 teaspoon cracked black
   peppercorns
6 (900g) beef eye fillet steaks
125g butter
1 tablespoon capers
2 teaspoons Worcestershire sauce
1 tablespoon chopped fresh parsley

Combine oysters, juice and pepper in small bowl, stand 10 minutes. Cut small pocket in side of each steak; insert 2 oysters in each pocket, secure with toothpick. Cook steaks in heated oiled griddle pan (or grill or barbecue) until browned both sides and cooked as desired. Remove from pan; cover to keep warm.

Beat butter in small bowl with electric mixer until light and creamy; beat in remaining ingredients. Spoon or pipe mixture onto steaks.

Serves 6.
- Best made just before serving. Butter can be prepared 2 days ahead.
- Storage: Butter covered, in refrigerator.
- Freeze: Butter suitable.
- Microwave: Not suitable.

OPPOSITE: Spicy Kebabs with Fruity Couscous.
ABOVE: Carpetbag Steak.

47

BEEF SATAYS

Soak bamboo skewers in water overnight to prevent burning. Beef rib eye roast is also known as whole Scotch fillet.

750g whole piece beef rib eye roast
3/4 cup (110g) unsalted roasted peanuts
1 tablespoon chopped fresh lemon grass
2 cloves garlic, chopped
2 teaspoons sambal oelek
1 teaspoon coarsely grated fresh ginger
1 tablespoon fresh coriander leaves
2 tablespoons honey
1 tablespoon fish sauce
1/2 cup (125ml) coconut cream

Cut rib eye into 2cm cubes, thread onto 12 skewers.

Blend or process remaining ingredients until peanuts are finely chopped. Place satays in large shallow dish, pour peanut mixture over; cover, refrigerate 3 hours or overnight.

Drain satays over medium bowl; reserve marinade. Place satays on wire rack, grill until browned all over and cooked as desired, brushing with reserved marinade during cooking.

Serves 4.

■ Can be marinated 2 days ahead.
■ Storage: Covered, in refrigerator.
■ Freeze: Uncooked marinated satays suitable.
■ Microwave: Not suitable.

VEAL MARSALA

8 (800g) veal leg schnitzels
plain flour
2 tablespoons vegetable oil
20g butter
1/3 cup (80ml) Marsala
3/4 cup (180ml) cream
1/2 teaspoon cracked black peppercorns
2 tablespoons chopped fresh chives

Toss schnitzels in flour; shake off excess. Heat oil and butter in large pan; cook schnitzels, in batches, until browned both sides and cooked as desired. Remove schnitzels from pan, cover to keep warm.

Drain fat from pan. Add remaining ingredients to pan; simmer, stirring, until sauce thickens slightly. Return schnitzels and any juices to pan, coat with sauce; serve immediately.

Serves 4.

■ Best made just before serving.
■ Freeze: Not suitable.
■ Microwave: Not suitable.

ABOVE LEFT: Beef Satays.
LEFT: Veal Marsala.
OPPOSITE: Hearty Tomato and Meatball Soup.

Plate, cutlery, placemat and napkin from Home & Garden on the Mall; glass plate from Mosman Storehouse

HEARTY TOMATO AND MEATBALL SOUP

500g minced beef
1 tablespoon tomato paste
2 cloves garlic, crushed
1 tablespoon chopped fresh
    coriander leaves
2 teaspoons ground cumin
2 teaspoons ground coriander
1 tablespoon vegetable oil
2 large (400g) onions, sliced
2 tablespoons plain flour
2 large (600g) potatoes, chopped
1 medium (120g) carrot, sliced
1/3 cup (80ml) tomato paste, extra
2 litres (8 cups) beef stock
2 large (500g) tomatoes,
    seeded, chopped
5 green onions, chopped

Combine mince, paste, garlic, fresh coriander with half the ground cumin and coriander in large bowl; shape level tablespoons of mixture into balls.

Heat oil in large pan, add onions; cook, stirring, until onions are soft. Stir in flour, then remaining ground cumin and coriander, potatoes, carrot and extra tomato paste. Gradually stir in stock; simmer, uncovered, 30 minutes. Add meatballs, simmer, uncovered, until meatballs and potatoes are cooked through. Stir in tomatoes and green onions, stir until heated through.

Serves 4 to 6.

■ Meatballs can be prepared
   2 hours ahead.
■ Storage: Covered, in refrigerator.
■ Freeze: Not suitable.
■ Microwave: Not suitable.

GARLIC MUSTARD STEAKS

Boneless sirloin steak is also known as New York cut.

4 (1kg) boneless sirloin steaks
4 cloves garlic, crushed
2 tablespoons seeded mustard
1 tablespoon chopped fresh
   thyme leaves
50g butter
1 tablespoon lemon juice
4 medium (300g) egg
   tomatoes, sliced

Spread steaks with combined garlic and mustard, sprinkle with half the thyme. Cook steaks, in batches, in heated oiled griddle pan (or grill or barbecue) until browned both sides and cooked as desired. Melt butter in large pan, add remaining thyme, juice and tomatoes; cook until tomatoes begin to soften. Top steaks with tomato mixture.

Serves 4.

■ Best made just before serving.
■ Freeze: Not suitable.
■ Microwave: Tomatoes suitable.

THAI-STYLE BEEF AND SPINACH STIR-FRY

Beef strips can be prepared from blade, fillet, rib eye, round, rump, sirloin or topside.

2 tablespoons peanut oil
2 medium (300g) onions, sliced
3 cloves garlic, crushed
1 tablespoon grated fresh ginger
1 large (350g) red capsicum, sliced
500g beef strips
1 bunch (500g) English spinach
1/2 cup firmly packed fresh
   mint leaves
1/3 cup (50g) chopped unsalted
   peanuts, toasted
1 tablespoon chopped fresh
   lemon grass
2 fresh kaffir lime leaves, shredded
2 teaspoons sugar
1 tablespoon fish sauce
1/4 cup (60ml) lime juice
1/2 teaspoon sesame oil

Heat half the oil in wok or large pan, add onions, garlic and ginger; stir-fry until onions are just soft. Add capsicum; stir-fry until just soft; remove from wok. Heat remaining oil in wok; stir-fry beef strips, in batches, until browned and almost cooked. Add spinach, mint, peanuts, vegetable mixture and remaining ingredients; stir-fry until spinach is just wilted and mixture is heated through.

Serves 4.

■ Best made just before serving.
■ Freeze: Not suitable.
■ Microwave: Not suitable.

LEFT: Garlic Mustard Steaks.
OPPOSITE: Thai-Style Beef and Spinach Stir-Fry.

Metal basket from Grace Bros

Plates from The Bay Tree Kitchen Shop

PORT STEAKS WITH GRILLED FIGS

Boneless sirloin steak is also known as New York cut.

**6 (1.2kg) boneless beef
  sirloin steaks**
1½ cups (375ml) port
1 cup (250ml) orange juice
**2 teaspoons cracked black
  peppercorns**
2 tablespoons seeded mustard
3 dried bay leaves
6 large (480g) fresh figs, halved

Combine steaks, port, juice, peppercorns, mustard and bay leaves in large shallow dish; cover, refrigerate 6 hours or overnight.

Drain steaks over medium pan, then simmer the marinade, uncovered, about 20 minutes or until marinade thickens slightly. Meanwhile, cook steaks, in batches, in heated oiled griddle pan (or grill or barbecue) until browned both sides and cooked as desired. Remove from pan; cover to keep warm. Cook figs in same pan until browned and softened slightly. Serve sauce over steaks; top with figs.

Serves 6.

■ Steaks best prepared a day ahead.
■ Storage: Covered, in refrigerator.
■ Freeze: Uncooked marinated
  steaks suitable.
■ Microwave: Not suitable.

MEDITERRANEAN-STYLE BEEF STIR-FRY

Beef strips can be prepared from blade, fillet, rib eye, round, rump, sirloin or topside.

2 medium (400g) red capsicums
2 medium (400g) yellow capsicums
¼ cup (60ml) vegetable oil
1kg beef strips
1 large (300g) red onion, sliced
3 cloves garlic, crushed
**¼ cup (35g) drained sun-dried
  tomatoes, sliced**
**⅓ cup firmly packed fresh basil
  leaves, shredded**
**1 bunch (500g) English
  spinach, shredded**
¼ cup (60ml) tomato paste
¼ cup water
1 tablespoon balsamic vinegar
1 teaspoon beef stock powder
250g fetta cheese, chopped

Quarter capsicums, remove seeds and membranes. Roast under grill or in very hot oven, skin side up, until skin blisters and blackens. Cover capsicum pieces in plastic or paper for 5 minutes, peel away skin, cut into 2cm slices.

Heat half the oil in wok or large pan; stir-fry beef strips, in batches, until browned and almost cooked; remove from wok. Heat remaining oil in wok, add onion and garlic; stir-fry until soft. Return beef to wok with capsicum, tomatoes, basil, spinach, paste, water, vinegar and stock powder; stir-fry until spinach is wilted. Gently stir in fetta.

Serves 6.

■ Best made just before serving.
■ Freeze: Not suitable.
■ Microwave: Not suitable.

BLACK BEAN BEEF AND ASPARAGUS

Beef strips can be prepared from blade, fillet, rib eye, round, rump, sirloin or topside.

1kg beef strips
1 tablespoon rice vinegar
1 tablespoon soy sauce
1 tablespoon dry sherry
2 cloves garlic, crushed
2 tablespoons peanut oil
1½ tablespoons salted dried black beans
2 medium (300g) onions, thickly sliced
2 bunches (500g) asparagus, halved
1 teaspoon cornflour
2 tablespoons oyster sauce
⅓ cup (80ml) beef stock

Combine beef strips with vinegar, sauce, sherry and garlic in medium bowl; cover, refrigerate for 2 hours or overnight.

Heat half the oil in wok or large pan; stir-fry beef mixture, in batches, until browned and almost cooked; remove from wok.

Rinse beans, drain, mash with fork. Heat remaining oil in wok, add beans, onions and asparagus; stir-fry until onions are almost soft. Return beef to wok, stir in blended cornflour, oyster sauce and stock; stir until mixture boils and thickens slightly.

Serves 6.

■ Can be prepared a day ahead.
■ Storage: Covered, in refrigerator.
■ Freeze: Uncooked, marinated beef strips suitable.
■ Microwave: Not suitable.

Plate and bowl from Ventura Design

Wrought iron tray from Bayteak Leisure Store

Setting from Orson & Blake Collectables

OPPOSITE: Port Steaks with Grilled Figs.
ABOVE RIGHT: Mediterranean-Style Beef Stir-Fry.
RIGHT: Black Bean Beef and Asparagus.

Traditional Favourites

Hearty beef meals are always a favourite with family and friends, and we've taken the recipes you love and combined them in one easy-to-follow section that you will refer to time and time again. Whether you're cooking a weeknight dinner or a meal for a special occasion, our delicious range of recipes offers roasts, casseroles, pies and many more that are guaranteed to satisfy every appetite.

BEEF RAGOUT

Beef round steak, skirt steak and gravy beef are also suitable for this recipe. Gravy beef is also known as boneless shin.

1kg beef chuck steak
plain flour
¼ cup (60ml) olive oil
2 cloves garlic, crushed
100g sliced pancetta, chopped
1½ cups (375ml) dry red wine
½ cup (125ml) beef stock
1½ tablespoons tomato paste
1 tablespoon Dijon mustard
1 tablespoon chopped fresh
  thyme leaves
4 medium (480g) carrots,
  roughly chopped
1 bunch (450g) spring onions,
  halved

Cut steak into 3cm cubes. Toss steak in flour; shake off excess. Heat half the oil in large pan; cook steak, in batches, until browned; remove from pan. Heat remaining oil in same pan, add garlic and pancetta; cook, stirring, until pancetta is crisp. Return steak to pan with wine, stock, paste, mustard, thyme and carrots, simmer, covered, 1¾ hours. Add onions, simmer, covered, 15 minutes.

Serves 6.

▓ Can be made a day ahead.
▓ Storage: Covered, in refrigerator.
▓ Freeze: Suitable.
▓ Microwave: Not suitable.

Tray from Bondi Storehouse

Plate and jug from Bondi Storehouse

Pewter bowl from Home & Garden on the Mall; plates from Royal Doulton

STANDING RIB ROAST WITH LEMON AND GARLIC

Order standing beef rib roast in advance from the butcher.

2kg standing beef rib roast
3/4 cup (180ml) lemon juice
1/3 cup (80ml) olive oil
6 cloves garlic, chopped
2 tablespoons chopped fresh
rosemary leaves
4 lemons
1 bulb (70g) garlic
4 sprigs fresh rosemary
1 cup (250ml) beef stock
1 cup (250ml) water
1 tablespoon cornflour
1 tablespoon water, extra

Place roast in large bowl, pour combined juice, oil, garlic and chopped rosemary all over roast. Cover; refrigerate 3 hours or overnight, turning the roast occasionally.

Drain roast over medium bowl; discard marinade. Cut each lemon into 6 wedges. Break garlic bulb into separate cloves; do not peel cloves.

Combine lemons, garlic and rosemary in large oiled baking dish. Place roast on lemon mixture, bake, uncovered, in moderate oven about 1½ hours or until roast is cooked as desired. Remove roast from dish, cover; stand 20 minutes. Remove lemons and garlic from dish, drain on absorbent paper; cover.

Meanwhile, drain fat from baking dish, reserve any pan juices; return juices to dish with stock and water. Cook, stirring, until mixture boils. Stir in blended cornflour and extra water, cook, stirring, until sauce boils and thickens; strain. Serve roast with lemon wedges, garlic and sauce.

Serves 6.

▓ Can be prepared a day ahead.
▓ Storage: Covered, in refrigerator.
▓ Freeze: Not suitable.
▓ Microwave: Not suitable.

FILET MIGNON

6 (400g) bacon rashers
6 (750g) beef eye fillet steaks
2 tablespoons olive oil
80g butter
2 cloves garlic, crushed
300g button mushrooms, sliced

Remove rind from bacon. Wrap a bacon rasher around each steak, trim to fit; secure with toothpicks. Heat oil in medium pan; cook steaks, in batches, until browned both sides and cooked as desired. Remove steaks from pan; cover to keep warm. Melt butter in same pan, add garlic and mushrooms; cook, stirring, until mushrooms are just tender. Serve steaks topped with mushroom mixture.

Serves 6.

▓ Best made just before serving.
▓ Freeze: Not suitable.
▓ Microwave: Not suitable.

OPPOSITE: Standing Rib Roast with Lemon and Garlic.
ABOVE: Filet Mignon.

Dish, fabric, napkin and serving cutlery from David Jones, Chatswood

VEAL PAPRIKA

2kg veal stewing steak
1/3 cup (80ml) olive oil
2 medium (300g) onions, sliced
3 cloves garlic, crushed
1 tablespoon sweet paprika
2 x 400g cans tomatoes
1/4 cup (60ml) tomato paste
1/4 cup (60ml) sour cream

Cut steak into 3cm cubes. Heat oil in large pan; cook steak, in batches, until browned; remove from pan. Add onions and garlic to same pan; cook, stirring, until onions are soft. Add paprika; cook, stirring, until fragrant.

Return steak and any juices to pan, add undrained crushed tomatoes and paste; simmer, covered, 1 hour. Then simmer, uncovered, about 20 minutes or until steak is tender and mixture thickens; stir in sour cream.

Serves 4 to 6.

■ Can be made a day ahead.
■ Storage: Covered, in refrigerator.
■ Freeze: Without sour cream, suitable.
■ Microwave: Not suitable.

BEEF AND BEAN BURRITOS

4 x 25cm round flour tortillas
1 cup (125g) grated tasty
    cheddar cheese
1 teaspoon ground hot paprika
3/4 cup (180ml) sour cream
1 tablespoon chopped fresh
    coriander leaves

BEEF FILLING
1 tablespoon olive oil
500g minced beef
1 medium (150g) onion,
    finely chopped
1 clove garlic, crushed
400g can tomatoes
35g packet taco seasoning mix
1/2 cup (125ml) water
300g can red kidney beans,
    rinsed, drained

GUACAMOLE
1 large (320g) avocado
1 baby (25g) onion, finely chopped
2 teaspoons lemon juice
few drops Tabasco
1 small (130g) tomato,
    finely chopped

Reheat Beef Filling; divide among the tortillas, roll up; secure with toothpicks. Place tortilla rolls on oiled oven tray; sprinkle with cheddar and paprika. Bake in moderately hot oven for about 10 minutes or until heated through. Serve Burritos topped with Guacamole, sour cream and coriander.

Beef Filling: Heat oil in medium pan, add mince; cook, stirring, until browned. Add onion and garlic; cook, stirring, until onion is soft. Add undrained crushed tomatoes and remaining ingredients, simmer, uncovered, about 15 minutes or until mixture thickens; cool.

Guacamole: Place avocado into medium bowl, mash with fork, stir in remaining ingredients.

Serves 4.

■ Beef Filling can be made a day ahead.
■ Storage: Covered, in refrigerator.
■ Freeze: Not suitable.
■ Microwave: Not suitable.

OPPOSITE: Beef and Bean Burritos.
ABOVE: Veal Paprika.

Platter and cactus from House In Newtown

Plate from Waterford Wedgwood; baking dish from David Jones, Chatswood

BRAWN

Gravy beef is also called boneless shin; osso bucco is shin with bone left in.

400g gravy beef
600g veal osso bucco
1 large (200g) onion, finely chopped
3 cloves garlic, crushed
1 large (180g) carrot, finely chopped
1.5 litres (6 cups) water
1 tablespoon gelatine
¼ cup water, extra
⅓ cup chopped fresh parsley

Oil 14cm x 21cm loaf pan; line base and 2 long sides with baking paper, allow paper to extend 3cm over sides.

Trim any fat from both gravy beef and osso bucco. Combine beef, osso bucco, onion, garlic, carrot and water in medium pan; simmer, covered, about

CANNELLONI

1 tablespoon olive oil
1 medium (150g) onion, finely chopped
2 cloves garlic, crushed
500g minced beef
⅓ cup (80ml) tomato paste
⅓ cup (80ml) water
120g packet (about 14) instant cannelloni shells
1 cup (125g) grated tasty cheddar cheese

TOMATO SAUCE
1 tablespoon olive oil
1 medium (150g) onion, finely chopped
2 cloves garlic, crushed
2 x 400g can tomatoes

CHEESE SAUCE
50g butter
¼ cup (35g) plain flour
3 cups (750ml) milk
1 cup (125g) grated tasty cheddar cheese

Oil 10 cup (2.5 litre) shallow ovenproof dish. Heat oil in medium pan, add onion and garlic; cook, stirring, until onion is soft. Add mince; cook, stirring, until

browned. Add paste and water; cook, stirring, about 5 minutes or until most of the liquid has evaporated; cool 10 minutes before filling shells.

Fill cannelloni shells with mince mixture. Spread half the Tomato Sauce over base of prepared dish, top with filled cannelloni, in single layer. Top with remaining Tomato Sauce, then Cheese Sauce. Sprinkle with cheddar; bake, uncovered, in moderately hot oven, about 35 minutes or until browned lightly.

Tomato Sauce: Heat oil in medium pan, add onion and garlic; cook, stirring, until onion is soft. Add undrained crushed tomatoes, simmer, uncovered, about 10 minutes or until sauce thickens, stirring occasionally.

Cheese Sauce: Melt butter in medium pan, stir in flour; cook, stirring, until bubbling. Remove from heat, gradually stir in milk. Cook, stirring, until sauce boils and thickens. Remove from heat, stir in cheddar.

Serves 4 to 6.

■ Can be made a day ahead.
■ Storage: Covered, in refrigerator.
■ Freeze: Not suitable.
■ Microwave: Cheese sauce suitable.

2 hours or until osso bucco meat is falling away from bone. Skim surface occasionally during cooking.

Strain beef mixture into large bowl; reserve 3 cups (750ml) of the stock. Remove meat from bones, discard bones; chop all meat finely. Combine reserved stock, meat and vegetables in large bowl. Sprinkle gelatine over extra water in small jug, stand in pan of simmering water, stir until dissolved. Stir gelatine mixture into meat mixture, then stir in parsley; cool. Pour mixture into prepared pan and cover; refrigerate overnight or until set.

Serves 6 to 8.

■ Must be made a day ahead.
■ Storage: Covered, in refrigerator.
■ Freeze: Not suitable.
■ Microwave: Gelatine suitable.

BEEF POT ROAST WITH BABY ONIONS

2kg corner piece beef topside roast
12 cloves garlic, peeled
2 tablespoons olive oil
10 (250g) baby onions
4 (250g) bacon rashers, chopped
1/3 cup (80ml) tomato paste
400g can tomatoes
1/4 cup (60ml) red wine vinegar
2 cups (500ml) beef stock
2 tablespoons Worcestershire sauce
2 tablespoons chopped fresh flat-leaf parsley

Make 12 deep cuts in top of roast; insert a garlic clove in each cut. Heat half the oil in large pan, add roast; cook until well browned all over, remove from pan.

Heat remaining oil in same pan, add onions and bacon; cook, stirring, until bacon is crisp. Add paste, undrained crushed tomatoes, vinegar, stock and sauce; bring to boil. Return roast to pan, simmer, covered, about 2 hours or until roast is tender; turn roast halfway during cooking.

Remove roast from pan; cover to keep warm. Boil tomato mixture in pan, uncovered, about 10 minutes or until mixture thickens; stir in parsley. Serve roast with tomato and onion mixture.

Serves 8.

■ Best made just before serving.
■ Storage: Covered, in refrigerator.
■ Freeze: Not suitable.
■ Microwave: Not suitable.

FAR LEFT: Cannelloni.
LEFT: Brawn.
ABOVE: Beef Pot Roast with Baby Onions.

Knife from Bondi Storehouse

STEAK AND KIDNEY PUDDING

Order about 250g fresh beef suet in advance from the butcher. Beef skirt steak, chuck steak and gravy beef are also suitable. Gravy beef is also known as boneless shin.

350g veal kidneys
2 teaspoons coarse cooking salt
1kg beef round steak
1/4 cup (60ml) vegetable oil
1 large (200g) onion, chopped
2 cloves garlic, crushed
150g mushrooms, chopped
1/4 cup (35g) plain flour
1/4 cup (60ml) tomato paste
2 cups (500ml) beef stock
2 tablespoons Worcestershire sauce
2 tablespoons chopped fresh parsley

SUET PASTRY
250g fresh beef suet
2 1/4 cups (335g) self-raising flour
3/4 cup (180ml) water, approximately

Place kidneys in small bowl, cover with water, add salt; cover, refrigerate for 4 hours or overnight.

Drain kidneys; discard the liquid. Remove fat and sinew from kidneys; slice thinly. Cut steak into 2cm cubes. Heat 1 tablespoon of the oil in large pan; cook steak, in batches, until browned; remove from pan. Heat remaining oil in pan, add onion, garlic and mushrooms; cook, stirring, until onion is soft. Stir in flour and paste; cook, stirring, until bubbling. Gradually stir in stock and sauce, cook, stirring, until sauce boils and thickens. Return steak and any juices to pan; simmer, covered, 45 minutes, stirring occasionally. Add kidneys; simmer, covered, 30 minutes or until steak is tender. Then simmer, uncovered, for about 10 minutes or until mixture thickens; cool.

Roll two-thirds of Suet Pastry large enough to line oiled 7 cup (1.75 litre) pudding steamer. Stir parsley into steak and kidney mixture; spoon into pastry case. Roll remaining pastry large enough to cover mixture. Lightly brush pastry edge with water, lift pastry onto mixture, trim edge; press edge to seal.

Cover pudding with double layer of oiled foil; secure with string or lid. Place steamer in large pan with enough boiling water to come halfway up side of steamer. Boil, covered, 3 hours. Replenish water with boiling water during cooking time. Remove pudding from water; stand 10 minutes before turning out.

Suet Pastry: Trim and discard membranes from suet, grate suet finely; you need 1 1/4 cups (100g). Sift flour into large bowl, add suet and enough water to mix to a soft dough. Knead dough on lightly floured surface until smooth; refrigerate 30 minutes.

Serves 8.

▦ Steak and kidney mixture best made a day ahead. Suet Pastry can be made a day ahead.
▦ Storage: Covered, in refrigerator.
▦ Freeze: Steak mixture suitable.
▦ Microwave: Not suitable.

Basket from House In Newtown

OSSO BUCCO

1.5kg (about 10) veal osso bucco
plain flour
2 tablespoons olive oil
2 medium (300g) onions, chopped
3 cloves garlic, crushed
1 tablespoon plain flour, extra
1/3 cup (80ml) tomato paste
2 cups (500ml) beef stock
3/4 cup (180ml) dry white wine
425g can tomatoes
4 bay leaves
1 large (180g) carrot, chopped
2 sticks celery, chopped
1 tablespoon grated lemon rind
1 tablespoon chopped
** fresh parsley**

Toss osso bucco in flour; shake off excess. Heat half the oil in large pan; cook osso bucco, in batches, until browned all over; remove from pan.

Heat remaining oil in pan, add onions and garlic; cook, stirring, until onions are soft. Stir in extra flour and paste; cook, stirring, until bubbling. Stir in stock, wine, undrained crushed tomatoes and bay leaves. Return osso bucco to pan, simmer, covered, 1¼ hours. Stir in carrot and celery, simmer, uncovered, about 20 minutes or until osso bucco and vegetables are tender.

Serve Osso Bucco sprinkled with rind and parsley.

Serves 6.
- Can be made a day ahead.
- Storage: Covered, in refrigerator.
- Freeze: Suitable.
- Microwave: Not suitable.

OPPOSITE: Steak and Kidney Pie.
ABOVE: Osso Bucco.

Plate and glasses from Waterford Wedgwood

BEEF RIB ROAST WITH GARLIC HERB BUTTER

Order standing beef rib roast in advance from the butcher.

2 tablespoons olive oil
2kg standing beef rib roast
2 teaspoons seasoned pepper
1 tablespoon olive oil
1 tablespoon balsamic vinegar

GARLIC HERB BUTTER
125g butter
2 cloves garlic, crushed
**2 tablespoons chopped
   fresh parsley**
**2 tablespoons chopped fresh
   mint leaves**
1 tablespoon white wine vinegar

Heat oil in large pan, add roast; cook until browned all over. Remove from pan, place on wire rack in baking dish, sprinkle with pepper; bake, uncovered, in moderately hot oven 1 hour. Brush roast with combined oil and vinegar; bake about another 10 minutes or until cooked as desired. Serve Beef Rib Roast with Garlic Herb Butter.
Garlic Herb Butter: Melt butter in small pan, add garlic and herbs, bring to boil. Remove from heat; stir in vinegar.

Serves 4 to 6.
■ Best made just before serving.
■ Freeze: Not suitable.
■ Microwave: Garlic Herb
  Butter suitable.

CORNED SILVERSIDE WITH PARSLEY SAUCE

**1.5kg whole piece beef
   corned silverside**
2 bay leaves
6 whole black peppercorns
1 large (200g) onion, quartered
1 large (180g) carrot, chopped
1 tablespoon brown malt vinegar
1/4 cup brown sugar

PARSLEY SAUCE
30g butter
1/4 cup (35g) plain flour
2 1/2 cups (625ml) milk
**1/3 cup (40g) grated tasty
   cheddar cheese**
1/3 cup chopped fresh parsley
1 tablespoon mild mustard

Combine silverside, bay leaves, peppercorns, onion, carrot, vinegar and half the sugar in large pan. Add enough water to just cover silverside; simmer, covered about 2 hours or until silverside is tender. Cool silverside for 1 hour in liquid in pan.

Remove silverside from pan; discard liquid. Sprinkle sheet of foil with the remaining sugar, wrap silverside in foil, stand 20 minutes before serving. Serve with Parsley Sauce.

Parsley Sauce: Melt butter in small pan, add flour; cook, stirring, until bubbling. Gradually stir in milk; cook, stirring, until sauce boils and thickens. Remove from heat; stir in cheddar, parsley and mustard.

Serves 4.
■ Corned Beef Silverside best made just before serving. Parsley Sauce can be made a day ahead.
■ Storage: Covered, in refrigerator.
■ Freeze: Not suitable.
■ Microwave: Sauce suitable.

OPPOSITE: Beef Rib Roast with Garlic Herb Butter.
ABOVE: Corned Silverside with Parsley Sauce.

AUSSIE BEEF CURRY

Beef chuck steak, skirt steak and gravy beef are also suitable for this recipe. Gravy beef is also known as boneless shin.

1kg beef round steak
1 tablespoon vegetable oil
1 large (200g) onion, chopped
1 tablespoon grated fresh ginger
1 tablespoon curry powder
½ teaspoon ground turmeric
½ teaspoon ground coriander
3 cups (750ml) beef stock
2 medium (300g) apples,
   peeled, chopped
2 tablespoons fruit chutney
1 tablespoon desiccatedcoconut
½ cup (80g) sultanas
¼ cup chopped fresh
   coriander leaves

BANANA SAMBAL
2 medium (400g) bananas, sliced
1 teaspoon lemon juice
½ cup (45g) desiccated coconut

Green glass from The Bay Tree Kitchen Shop

Bowls and plates from Accoutrement; basket from Morris Home & Garden Wares

BEEF WELLINGTON

We used beef fillet from the rump here; it's also known as butt fillet.

800g whole piece beef butt fillet
1 tablespoon olive oil
375g block frozen puff pastry,
   thawed
1 egg, lightly beaten

MUSHROOM TOPPING
30g butter
1 small (80g) onion, finely chopped
300g button mushrooms,
   finely chopped
2 tablespoons dry red wine
1 tablespoon Worcestershire sauce
2 teaspoons plain flour

BROWN ONION SAUCE
2 teaspoons olive oil
1 small (80g) onion, finely chopped
⅓ cup (80ml) dry red wine
1½ cups (375ml) beef stock

Tie fillet with string at 3cm intervals. Heat oil in large pan, add fillet; cook until well browned all over. Transfer fillet to oiled oven tray, bake in moderately hot oven 10 minutes; cool.

Remove string from fillet, spread Mushroom Topping all over fillet. Roll pastry on floured surface until it forms 28cm x 40cm rectangle. Cut pastry into 28cm square; cut remaining pastry into leaf shapes. Lightly brush edges of pastry square with egg. Wrap pastry around fillet, press edges to seal, place seam side down on oiled oven tray. Decorate with pastry leaves; brush with remaining egg. Bake in hot oven for 10 minutes, reduce heat to moderate, bake another 20 minutes or until pastry is golden brown. Serve Beef Wellington with Brown Onion Sauce.

Mushroom Topping: Melt butter in medium pan, add onion; cook, stirring, until onion is soft. Add mushrooms, wine and sauce; cook, stirring, until mushrooms are soft and all liquid has evaporated. Add flour; cook, stirring, until mixture thickens; cool.

Brown Onion Sauce: Heat oil in small pan, add onion; cook, stirring, until onion is browned lightly; stir in wine, simmer, uncovered, 2 minutes. Add stock, simmer, uncovered, 10 minutes or until sauce thickens slightly.

Serves 4.

■ Mushroom Topping can be made a day ahead.
■ Storage: Covered, in refrigerator.
■ Freeze: Not suitable.
■ Microwave: Not suitable.

Cut steak into 3cm cubes. Heat oil in large pan; cook steak, in batches, until browned; remove from pan. Add onion, ginger, curry powder and spices to same pan; cook, stirring, until onion is soft. Return steak to pan with stock, apples, chutney, coconut and sultanas, simmer, covered, 1 hour. Then simmer, uncovered, about 30 minutes or until steak is tender and sauce thickens. Stir in coriander. Serve with Banana Sambal.

Banana Sambal: Combine banana and juice in small bowl; add coconut.

Serves 4.

▨ Aussie Curry can be made a day ahead. Banana Sambal best made just before serving.
▨ Storage: Curry, covered, in refrigerator.
▨ Freeze: Not suitable.
▨ Microwave: Not suitable.

Platter and Pillivuyt dish from Kitchen Kapers

VEAL AND MUSHROOM FRICASSEE

1kg veal stewing steak
20g butter
1 medium (350g) leek, sliced
1 clove garlic, crushed
½ cup (125ml) dry white wine
2½ cups (625ml) chicken stock
2 bay leaves
250g button mushrooms, sliced
2 teaspoons chopped fresh
    oregano leaves
½ cup (125ml) cream
2 tablespoons lemon juice
2 egg yolks

Cut steak into 3cm cubes. Melt butter in large pan; cook steak, in batches, until browned; remove from pan. Add leek and garlic to same pan; cook, stirring, until leek is soft. Return steak to pan with wine, stock and bay leaves; simmer, covered, about 1 hour or until steak is tender. Stir in mushrooms and oregano; simmer, uncovered, for about 15 minutes. Just before serving, stir in cream, lemon juice and egg yolks; cook, stirring, without boiling, until just heated through.

Serves 4 to 6.

▨ Can be prepared a day ahead.
▨ Storage: Covered, in refrigerator.
▨ Freeze: Suitable.
▨ Microwave: Not suitable.

OPPOSITE: Beef Wellington.
LEFT: Aussie Beef Curry.
ABOVE: Veal and Mushroom Fricassee.

SPICED MOROCCAN BEEF

Be sure to buy fresh beef brisket, not corned or salted beef brisket.

1 teaspoon coriander seeds, crushed
½ teaspoon cumin seeds
2kg fresh rolled beef brisket
¼ cup (60ml) olive oil
1 large (200g) onion, chopped
4 cloves garlic, crushed
2 teaspoons sambal oelek
2 teaspoons ground cumin
2 teaspoons ground coriander
¼ cup (35g) plain flour
1 litre (4 cups) beef stock
2 teaspoons grated lemon rind

CHICKPEA COUSCOUS
2 cups (400g) couscous
2 cups (500ml) boiling water
50g butter, chopped
300g can chickpeas, rinsed, drained
2 large (500g) tomatoes, chopped

Sprinkle coriander and cumin seeds over brisket. Heat 1 tablespoon of the oil in deep flameproof baking dish, add brisket; cook until well browned all over, remove from dish.

Heat remaining oil in dish, add onion and garlic; cook, stirring, until onion is soft. Add sambal oelek, ground cumin and coriander; cook, stirring, until fragrant. Stir in flour; cook, stirring, until bubbling; gradually stir in stock and rind, bring to boil, stirring. Return brisket to dish, cover dish with foil; bake in moderately slow oven about 3 hours or until brisket is tender. Turn brisket halfway during baking.

Remove brisket from dish; cover to keep warm. Boil sauce, uncovered, on cooktop, stirring occasionally, about 20 minutes or until sauce thickens. Serve brisket with Chickpea Couscous and sauce.
Chickpea Couscous: Combine couscous, water, butter and chickpeas in large bowl, cover, stand about 5 minutes or until water is absorbed; stir in chopped tomatoes.

Serves 8.

■ Best made just before serving.
■ Freeze: Not suitable.
■ Microwave: Not suitable.

OPPOSITE: Cottage Pie.
LEFT: Spiced Moroccan Beef.

COTTAGE PIE

2 teaspoons olive oil
1kg minced beef
1 medium (150g) onion, chopped
1 medium (120g) carrot, chopped
1 stick celery, chopped
1 tablespoon chopped fresh
thyme leaves
2 cups (500ml) beef stock
1 tablespoon Worcestershire sauce
¼ cup (60ml) tomato paste
½ cup (60g) frozen peas

POTATO TOPPING
6 medium (1.2kg) potatoes,
chopped
40g butter
¼ cup (60ml) milk, approximately

Heat oil in large pan, add mince and onion; cook, stirring until mince is browned. Add carrot, celery, thyme, stock, sauce and paste; simmer, uncovered, about 30 minutes or until carrots are tender. Add peas; cook, uncovered 10 minutes or until peas are tender and sauce thickens. Spoon mixture into 10 cup (2.5 litre) ovenproof dish. Pipe or spread Potato Topping over mince mixture. Bake, uncovered, in moderate oven about 30 minutes or until browned and heated through.

Potato Topping: Boil, steam or microwave potatoes until tender; drain. Push potatoes through coarse sieve; stir in butter and enough milk to make a smooth consistency.

Serves 4 to 6.

- Can be made a day ahead.
- Storage: Covered, in refrigerator.
- Freeze: Suitable.
- Microwave: Not suitable.

White platter, tray, placemat, napkin, salt and pepper shaker from Corso De' Fiori

ROAST BEEF

2kg corner piece beef topside roast
2 cups (500ml) dry red wine
2 bay leaves
6 black peppercorns
1/4 cup (60ml) seeded mustard
4 cloves garlic, sliced
4 sprigs fresh thyme
1 medium (150g) onion, chopped
2 medium (240g) carrots, roughly chopped
1 large (500g) leek, roughly chopped
2 sticks celery, roughly chopped
2 tablespoons olive oil
2 tablespoons plain flour
1 1/2 cups (375ml) beef stock

Combine roast, wine, bay leaves, peppercorns, mustard, garlic, thyme and onion in large bowl; cover, refrigerate 3 hours or overnight.

Drain roast over medium bowl; reserve 1 cup (250ml) of marinade. Combine carrots, leek and celery in large baking dish, top with roast; brush roast with oil. Bake, uncovered, in moderate oven about 1 1/2 hours or until browned and cooked as desired.

Remove roast from pan, wrap in foil, stand for 20 minutes before serving. Remove vegetables with slotted spoon; discard vegetables. Pour pan juices into jug, stand 2 minutes, then pour off excess oil; reserve 1 1/2 tablespoons oil for Yorkshire Puddings and 2 tablespoons of pan juices for gravy.

Heat reserved pan juices for gravy in same baking dish, add flour; cook, stirring until bubbling. Gradually add reserved marinade and stock; cook, stirring, until mixture boils and thickens; strain gravy into jug. Serve with Roast Potatoes and Pumpkin, Yorkshire Puddings and gravy.

ROAST POTATOES AND PUMPKIN

4 medium (1.2kg) golden nugget pumpkins
1 tablespoons fresh thyme sprigs
1/3 cup (80ml) olive oil
6 large (1.8kg) potatoes, unpeeled, quartered
4 cloves garlic, unpeeled, bruised
2 tablespoons fresh rosemary sprigs
1 teaspoon coarse cooking salt

Quarter pumpkins, remove seeds. Combine pumpkins, thyme and half the oil in bowl. Combine remaining oil with potatoes, garlic, rosemary and salt in large baking dish; bake, uncovered, in moderate oven 30 minutes. Add pumpkin mixture; bake 45 minutes or until vegetables are cooked.

YORKSHIRE PUDDINGS

1 cup (150g) plain flour
1/2 teaspoon salt
2 eggs, lightly beaten
1/2 cup (125ml) milk
1/2 cup (125ml) water

Sift flour and salt into bowl, make well in centre, add combined eggs, milk and water all at once. Using wooden spoon, gradually stir in flour from side of bowl until batter is smooth. Cover; allow to stand 30 minutes.

Divide the reserved oil among 12-hole (2 tablespoons/40ml capacity) patty pan, heat in hot oven 2 minutes. Divide batter among pan holes. Bake about 15 minutes or until puddings are puffed and golden.

Serves 8.

■ Must be made just before serving.
■ Freeze: Not suitable.
■ Microwave: Not suitable.

CHILLI CON CARNE

Beef round steak, skirt steak and gravy beef are also suitable for this recipe. Gravy beef is also known as boneless shin.

1.5kg beef chuck steak
2 tablespoons vegetable oil
2 medium (300g) onions, sliced
2 medium (400g) red capsicums, chopped
3 cloves garlic, crushed
2 small fresh red chillies, finely chopped
2 teaspoons ground cumin
2 teaspoons ground coriander
1 teaspoon hot chilli powder
2 x 425g cans tomatoes
3/4 cup (180ml) tomato paste
1 1/4 cups (310ml) beef stock
300g can red kidney beans, rinsed, drained

Cut steak into 3cm cubes. Heat oil in pan; cook steak, in batches, until browned; remove from pan. Add onions, capsicums, garlic and chillies to same pan; cook, stirring until onions are soft and browned lightly. Add spices; cook, stirring until fragrant. Return steak and any juices to pan with undrained crushed tomatoes, paste and stock. Simmer, covered, 1 hour. Add beans; simmer, uncovered about 30 minutes or until steak is tender and sauce thickens.

Serves 4 to 6.

■ Can be made a day ahead.
■ Storage: Covered, in refrigerator.
■ Freeze: Suitable.
■ Microwave: Not suitable.

BELOW: Chilli Con Carne.
OPPOSITE: Deep Dish Pizza.

Plates, bowls and napkins from Accoutrement; olive oil trivet from The Bay Tree Kitchen Shop

DEEP DISH PIZZA

1 tablespoon (14g) dry yeast
2 teaspoons sugar
1 3/4 cups (430ml) warm water
4 1/2 cups (675g) plain flour
1 teaspoon salt
1/4 cup (60ml) olive oil
2 tablespoons olive oil, extra
1 medium (120g) zucchini
1 (60g) baby eggplant
2 1/2 cups (250g) grated mozzarella cheese
250g cherry tomatoes, halved
1/2 cup (60g) seeded black olives
1/4 cup small fresh basil leaves

TOMATO SAUCE

1 tablespoon olive oil
1 medium (150g) onion, sliced
3 cloves garlic, crushed
400g can tomatoes
½ cup (125ml) tomato paste
¼ cup (60ml) dry red wine

BEEF TOPPING

1 tablespoon olive oil
650g minced beef
1 teaspoon sweet paprika

Lightly oil 34cm round pizza tray. Whisk yeast, sugar, water and 2 tablespoons of the flour together in small bowl; cover, stand in warm place for about 10 minutes or until mixture is frothy.

Sift remaining flour and salt into large bowl, stir in yeast mixture and oil; mix to a soft dough. Knead dough on floured surface about 5 minutes or until smooth. Place dough in large oiled bowl, cover, stand in warm place about 1 hour or until doubled in size.

Roll dough on floured surface to 36cm round; lift onto prepared tray, tuck excess dough under to form rim. Brush rim with extra oil. Use a vegetable peeler to slice zucchini and eggplant.

Spread pizza base with Tomato Sauce, sprinkle with Beef Topping, half the mozzarella, zucchini, eggplant, tomatoes, olives and then remaining mozzarella. Bake in very hot oven about 20 minutes; reduce heat to moderate, bake another 25 minutes or until base is crisp. Serve sprinkled with basil leaves.

Tomato Sauce: Heat oil in medium pan, add onion and garlic; cook, stirring, until onion is soft. Stir in undrained crushed tomatoes, paste and wine, simmer, uncovered, about 5 minutes or until sauce thickens; cool.

Beef Topping: Heat oil in medium pan, add mince and paprika; cook, stirring, until browned; cool.

Serves 6 to 8.

- Tomato Sauce and Beef Topping can be made a day ahead.
- Storage: Covered, separately, in refrigerator.
- Freeze: Dough suitable.
- Microwave: Not suitable.

BEEF, PRUNE AND YOGURT TAGINE

Beef round steak, skirt steak and gravy beef are also suitable for this recipe. Gravy beef is also known as boneless shin.

1kg beef chuck steak
2 teaspoons coriander seeds
2 teaspoons cumin seeds
2 tablespoons plain flour
½ teaspoon cracked
  black peppercorns
¼ cup (60ml) olive oil
2 medium (300g) onions,
  finely chopped
4 cloves garlic, crushed
1 teaspoon ground allspice
½ teaspoon ground turmeric
¼ teaspoon chilli powder
1 cinnamon stick
½ cup (125ml) yogurt
1½ cups (375ml) beef stock
1½ tablespoons balsamic vinegar
4 strips lemon rind
1 cup (170g) seeded prunes
⅓ cup (55g) blanched almonds
2 teaspoons honey
1 tablespoon chopped fresh
  coriander leaves

STEAK AND KIDNEY PIE

Beef round, skirt and chuck steak are also suitable for this recipe. Gravy beef is also known as boneless shin.

250g beef kidney
2 teaspoons salt
1kg gravy beef
1 tablespoon vegetable oil
1 medium (170g) onion, sliced
¾ cup (180ml) beef stock
¼ cup (60ml) dry red wine
1 tablespoon soy sauce
¼ cup (35g) plain flour
⅓ cup (80ml) water
1 tablespoon chopped fresh parsley
2 sheets ready-rolled puff pastry
1 egg, lightly beaten

Remove skin and fat from kidney, place in bowl, cover with cold water, add salt; cover, refrigerate overnight.

Drain kidney, rinse under cold water; drain well. Cut kidney into thin slices; cut gravy beef into 3cm cubes. Heat oil in large pan; cook beef, in batches, until browned. Remove from pan. Add onion to same pan; cook, stirring until soft. Return beef and any juices to pan, add kidney, stock, wine and sauce; simmer, covered, about 1 hour or until beef is tender. Stir in blended flour and water, stir until mixture boils and thickens; stir in parsley. Transfer mixture to 6 cup (1.5 litre) ovenproof dish; cool for 10 minutes. Top with pastry sheet, trim to fit dish; brush with egg. Decorate pie with shapes cut from remaining pastry sheet; brush with egg. Make 2 small cuts in pastry; bake in moderate oven about 40 minutes or until browned.

Serves 6.

■ Can be prepared a day ahead.
■ Storage: Covered, in refrigerator.
■ Freeze: Gravy beef mixture suitable.
■ Microwave: Not suitable.

Cut steak into 3cm cubes. Add coriander and cumin seeds to heated dry pan, stir over heat until fragrant; crush in mortar and pestle.

Toss steak in combined flour and pepper. Heat 2 tablespoons of the oil in large pan; cook steak, in batches, until browned; remove from pan. Heat remaining oil in same pan, add onions, garlic, spices, chilli powder, cinnamon stick and crushed seeds; cook, stirring, until onions are soft. Return steak to pan, stir in yogurt, 1 tablespoon at a time; cook, stirring well between additions. Add stock, vinegar and rind, simmer, covered, 1 hour. Add prunes, simmer, uncovered, 30 minutes, or until steak is tender. Discard cinnamon stick and rind. Stir in remaining ingredients.

Serves 6.

■ Can be made a day ahead.
■ Storage: Covered, in refrigerator.
■ Freeze: Not suitable.
■ Microwave: Not suitable.

Plates from Villeroy & Boch; glasses and placemat from Home & Garden on the Mall; carafe from House In Newtown

VEAL OSCAR

8 x 70g veal leg steaks
plain flour
1 tablespoon olive oil
1 bunch (250g) asparagus
12 (400g) uncooked king prawns

BEARNAISE SAUCE
1/3 cup white wine vinegar
1/4 teaspoon cracked
**   black peppercorns**
2 green onions, chopped
3 egg yolks
185g butter, melted
1 tablespoon chopped fresh
**   flat-leaf parsley**
2 teaspoons chopped fresh
**   tarragon leaves**

Toss steaks in flour; shake off excess. Heat oil in large pan; cook steak, in batches, until browned both sides and cooked as desired.

Meanwhile, boil, steam or microwave asparagus until just tender. Drain asparagus, cut in half lengthways; keep warm. Peel and devein prawns, leaving tails intact. Add prawns to pan of boiling water, boil until just cooked; drain. Serve steaks topped with asparagus, prawns and Bearnaise Sauce.

Bearnaise Sauce: Combine vinegar and peppercorns in small pan; simmer, uncovered, about 5 minutes or until liquid is reduced to 2 tablespoons. Strain into small bowl; reserve liquid. Place egg yolks in large bowl over pan of simmering water; do not allow water to touch base of bowl. Whisk in the reserved liquid, then gradually whisk in melted butter in a thin stream until mixture thickens slightly. Stir in herbs and serve immediately. Makes about 1 cup (250ml) sauce.

Serves 4.

■ Best made just before serving.
■ Freeze: Not suitable.
■ Microwave: Not suitable.

FAR LEFT: Steak and Kidney Pie.
LEFT: Beef, Prune and Yogurt Tagine.
ABOVE: Veal Oscar.

VITELLO TONNATO

Vitello Tonnato, or cold sliced veal with tuna sauce, is a classic Italian dish. Order a nut of veal in advance from the butcher; ask butcher to tie veal securely.

1 bunch (100g) fresh parsley
2 litres (8 cups) water,
    approximately
2 sticks celery, halved
1 medium (120g) carrot, halved
1 large (200g) onion, halved
3 bay leaves
2 teaspoons black peppercorns
1.2kg nut of veal
2 teaspoons capers

TUNA MAYONNAISE
2 egg yolks
1 tablespoon lemon juice
½ cup (125ml) olive oil
½ cup (125ml) vegetable oil
125g can tuna slices, drained
5 anchovy fillets, rinsed, drained
1½ tablespoons small capers
1½ tablespoons lemon juice, extra
¼ cup (60ml) milk

Chop enough parsley to give 1 tablespoon; reserve. Place water, celery, carrot, onion, bay leaves, peppercorns and remaining parsley in large pan, bring to boil. Add veal and more water if necessary to cover veal; simmer, covered, about 1½ hours or until veal is cooked through.

Remove pan from heat; stand for 30 minutes. Transfer veal and stock to large bowl, cover, refrigerate until cold. Remove veal from stock; discard stock; cut veal into thin slices. Spread half the Tuna Mayonnaise on serving plate, top with veal then cover with remaining Mayonnaise. Cover and refrigerate for 2 hours. Serve Vitello Tonnato sprinkled with reserved parsley and capers.

Tuna Mayonnaise: Blend or process egg yolks and juice until smooth. Add combined oils gradually in a thin stream while motor is operating, blend until mixture thickens. Add tuna, anchovies, capers, extra juice and milk, blend until smooth.

Serves 6 to 8.

■ Veal can be prepared a day ahead.
■ Storage: Veal, in stock, covered, in refrigerator.
■ Freeze: Not suitable.
■ Microwave: Not suitable.

CHEESY BEEF AND ANGEL HAIR LASAGNE

500g packet angel hair pasta
2 cups (600g) ricotta cheese
½ cup (40g) grated parmesan
    cheese
2 eggs, lightly beaten
¼ cup chopped fresh parsley
½ cup (60g) grated tasty
    cheddar cheese

MEAT SAUCE
2 tablespoons olive oil
2 medium (300g) onions, chopped
2 cloves garlic, crushed
1.5kg minced beef
½ cup (125ml) tomato paste
425g can tomatoes
1½ cups (375ml) beef stock
½ cup (125ml) dry red wine
2 tablespoons chopped
    fresh oregano

WHITE SAUCE
40g butter
¼ cup (35g) plain flour
2 cups (500ml) milk
1 teaspoon Dijon mustard
¼ teaspoon ground nutmeg

Add pasta to large pan of boiling water, boil, uncovered, about 3 minutes or until pasta is just tender; drain. Combine ricotta, parmesan, eggs and parsley in medium bowl. Spread a third of the meat sauce over base of 16 cup (4 litre) shallow ovenproof dish. Top with a third of the pasta and half the ricotta mixture. Repeat layering, finishing with pasta; pour white sauce over pasta, sprinkle with cheddar. Bake, uncovered, in moderate oven about 1 hour or until cheddar is melted and top browned.

Meat Sauce: Heat oil in pan, add onions, garlic and mince; cook, stirring, until mince is browned. Stir in paste, undrained crushed tomatoes, stock, wine and oregano; simmer, uncovered, about 45 minutes or until sauce thickens.

White Sauce: Melt butter in pan, stir in flour, stir over heat until bubbling. Remove from heat; gradually stir in milk, add mustard and nutmeg, stir over heat until sauce boils and thickens.

Serve 6.

■ Can be made a day ahead.
■ Storage: Covered, in refrigerator.
■ Freeze: Suitable.
■ Microwave: Pasta and White Sauce suitable.

OPPOSITE: Cheesy Beef and Angel Hair Lasagne.
LEFT: Vitello Tonnato.

Blue and white plates from The Bay Tree Kitchen Shop; fork from House In Newtown

Plate from Waterford Wedgwood; fork from The Bay Tree Kitchen Shop

ROAST BEEF AND VEGETABLES IN AN OVEN BAG

2 cloves garlic, peeled
1.8kg corner piece beef topside roast
6 small sprigs fresh thyme
6 medium (720g) carrots, halved
12 baby (300g) onions, peeled
1 tablespoon seeded mustard
¼ cup (60ml) honey
2 tablespoons olive oil

ITALIAN-STYLE POT ROAST

Be sure to buy fresh beef brisket, not corned or salted beef brisket.

2 tablespoons olive oil
2kg fresh rolled beef brisket
1 large (200g) onion, sliced
2 cloves garlic, crushed
2 baby (120g) eggplants, sliced
1 medium (200g) green capsicum, chopped
1 medium (200g) red capsicum, chopped
125g button mushrooms, halved
2 sprigs fresh oregano
2 x 425g cans tomatoes
¾ cup (180ml) tomato paste
3½ cups (875ml) beef stock
½ cup (60g) seeded black olives
1 tablespoon chopped fresh oregano, extra

Heat oil in pan, add brisket, cook until browned all over; remove from pan. Add onion, garlic, eggplants, capsicums and mushrooms to same pan; cook, stirring about 5 minutes or until vegetables are soft; remove from pan.

Return brisket and any juices to pan with the oregano sprigs, undrained crushed tomatoes, paste and stock. Simmer, covered, 1½ hours, turning occasionally. Return vegetables to pan with olives; simmer, uncovered, another 30 minutes or until brisket is tender and sauce thickens. Serve sprinkled with extra oregano leaves.

Serves 6.

■ Best made on day of serving.
■ Storage: Covered, in refrigerator.
■ Freeze: Not suitable.
■ Microwave: Not suitable.

Cut each garlic clove into 3 slices. Make 12 small cuts on fat side of roast; insert garlic and thyme into each cut.

Cut a narrow strip from the top of a 35cm x 48cm oven bag to use as a tie. Place roast, carrots and onions in bag. Add combined remaining ingredients to bag; close end with tie. Gently turn bag to coat roast and vegetables with mustard mixture. Place bag in large baking dish, pierce 3 holes near tie end. Bake in moderate oven about 1½ hours or until roast is cooked as desired. Remove roast and vegetables from bag; cover, keep warm. Pour juices from oven bag into baking dish, simmer, uncovered, until reduced to about ½ cup (125ml). Serve roast and vegetables drizzled with mustard mixture.

Serves 6.
- Best made just before serving.
- Freeze: Not suitable.
- Microwave: Not suitable.

OPPOSITE: Italian-Style Pot Roast.
BELOW: Roast Beef and Vegetables in an Oven Bag.

Plates from Royal Doulton; cutlery from Villeroy & Boch; placemat and napkin from Home & Garden on the Mall; grinder from House In Newtown

VEAL CORDON BLEU

8 (800g) veal schnitzels
200g Swiss cheese, sliced
200g sliced ham
plain flour
2 eggs, lightly beaten
1¼ cups (125g) packaged
  breadcrumbs
¼ cup (60ml) olive oil

Place veal between sheets of plastic wrap; pound with meat mallet until an even thickness. Place a slice of cheese and ham on half of each schnitzel, fold schnitzels over to enclose filling; press edges together. Toss schnitzels in flour, dip in eggs, then coat in bread-crumbs. Heat oil in large pan; cook schnitzels until browned both sides and cooked as desired.

Serves 6 to 8.

■ Can be prepared a day ahead.
■ Storage: Covered, in refrigerator.
■ Freeze: Not suitable.
■ Microwave: Not suitable.

VEAL MARENGO

¼ cup (60ml) olive oil
1.5kg veal stewing steak
2 medium (300g) onions, sliced
1 medium (350g) leek, sliced
4 cloves garlic, crushed
¼ cup (60ml) tomato paste
2 teaspoons grated orange rind
1 cup (250ml) dry white wine
1 cup (250ml) beef stock
300g button mushrooms
⅔ cup (160ml) orange juice
3 large (750g) tomatoes, peeled,
  seeded, chopped

Cut steak into 3cm cubes. Heat oil in large pan; cook steak, in batches, until well browned; remove from pan. Add onions, leek and garlic to same pan; cook, stirring, until onions are soft. Return steak and any juices to pan, add remaining ingredients, simmer, covered, 1 hour. Then simmer, uncovered, 45 minutes or until steak is tender and sauce thickens.

Serves 6.

■ Can be made a day ahead.
■ Storage: Covered, in refrigerator.
■ Freeze: Suitable.
■ Microwave: Not suitable.

Pan and pepper grinder from Bondi Storehouse

Basket from House In Newtown

ABOVE LEFT: Veal Cordon Bleu.
BELOW LEFT: Veal Marengo.
OPPOSITE: Beef Olives.

BEEF OLIVES

¼ cup (60ml) olive oil
1 small (80g) onion, finely chopped
2 cloves garlic, crushed
6 (400g) bacon rashers, finely
    chopped
1 small (150g) red capsicum,
    chopped
1 small (150g) green capsicum,
    chopped
125g button mushrooms, sliced
½ cup (35g) stale breadcrumbs
¼ cup (30g) seeded black olives,
    sliced
8 (650g) beef topside schnitzels
1 medium (150g) onion, chopped,
    extra
425g can tomato puree
1 tablespoon tomato paste
1 tablespoon balsamic vinegar
2 teaspoons sugar
1 cup (250ml) beef stock
1 tablespoon chopped fresh parsley

Heat half the oil in large pan, add onion, garlic and bacon; cook, stirring, until bacon is slightly crisp. Add capsicums and mushrooms; cook, stirring, until vegetables are soft. Remove from heat, stir in breadcrumbs and olives, remove from pan; cool.

Divide mixture into 8 portions, spoon a portion onto each schnitzel, roll up to enclose mixture; secure schnitzels with string or toothpicks.

Heat remaining oil in same pan; cook Beef Olives, in batches, until browned all over. Remove from pan, drain on absorbent paper; cover, keep warm. Add extra onion to pan; cook, stirring, until onion is soft. Add puree, paste, vinegar, sugar and stock, simmer, uncovered about 5 minutes or until mixture thickens; stir in parsley. Return Beef Olives and any juices to pan in single layer, simmer, covered, about 20 minutes or until cooked through.

Serves 4.
■ Can be made a day ahead.
■ Storage: Covered, in refrigerator.
■ Freeze: Suitable.
■ Microwave: Not suitable.

BOUEF BOURGUIGNONNE

Beef round steak, skirt steak and gravy beef are also suitable for this recipe. Gravy beef is also known as boneless shin.

2kg beef chuck steak
2 tablespoons olive oil
2 bunches (730g) spring onions, halved
4 cloves garlic, crushed
3 (200g) bacon rashers, chopped
300g button mushrooms
1/3 cup (80ml) tomato paste
2 cups (500ml) dry red wine
3/4 cup (180ml) port
1/2 cup (125ml) beef stock

Cut steak into 3cm cubes. Heat oil in pan; cook steak, in batches, until well browned, remove from pan. Add onions, garlic and bacon to same pan; cook, stirring, until onions are soft. Add steak and any juices with remaining ingredients; simmer, covered, about 1½ hours or until steak is tender. Then simmer, uncovered, another 45 minutes or until sauce thickens.

Serves 6.

■ Can be made a day ahead.
■ Storage: Covered, in refrigerator.
■ Freeze: Suitable.
■ Microwave: Not suitable.

BRAISED BEEF OXTAIL

2 teaspoons olive oil
2kg chopped beef oxtail
2 large (400g) onions, sliced
2 cloves garlic, crushed
2 teaspoons ground hot paprika
2 x 400g cans tomatoes
¼ cup (60ml) tomato paste
½ cup (125ml) dry red wine
4 cups (1 litre) beef stock
2 bay leaves
2 large (360g) carrots, chopped
¼ cup chopped fresh oregano
500g frozen broad beans, thawed, peeled

Heat oil in large pan; cook oxtail, in batches, until well browned. Remove from pan. Add onions, garlic and paprika to same pan; cook, stirring until onions are soft. Return oxtail to pan with undrained crushed tomatoes, paste, wine, stock, bay leaves and carrots; simmer, covered, 2 hours or until oxtail is tender. Cool mixture; cover, refrigerate overnight. Remove fat from surface of mixture before reheating. Stir in oregano and beans; cook, stirring, until beans are heated through.

Serves 8.

■ Must be made a day ahead.
■ Storage: Covered, in refrigerator.
■ Freeze: Suitable.
■ Microwave: Not Suitable.

OPPOSITE: Braised Beef Oxtail.
BELOW: Bouef Bourguignonne.

Casserole from Bondi Storehouse

Platter from Villeroy & Boch; glasses and napkin from Corso De' Fiori

ROAST BEEF WITH FRESH HERB SEASONING

Beef rib-eye roast is also known as whole scotch fillet.

40g butter
1 large (200g) onion, chopped
¼ cup chopped fresh parsley
2 teaspoons chopped fresh
    oregano leaves
2 teaspoons chopped fresh
    thyme leaves
2 cups (140g) stale breadcrumbs
1 egg yolk
1.5kg whole piece beef rib-eye roast
2 tablespoons olive oil
½ teaspoon coarse cooking salt
2 tablespoons plain flour
2 cups (500ml) beef stock

Melt butter in pan, add onion; cook, stirring, until onion is soft. Combine onion, herbs, breadcrumbs and egg yolk in medium bowl. Shape mixture into 2 rolls, each the length of the roast. Cover rolls with plastic wrap, freeze 1 hour or until frozen.

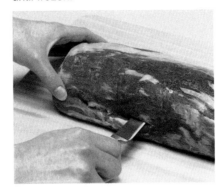

Cut a deep pocket in side of roast; insert both rolls of seasoning in pocket, secure with string. Place roast in baking dish, rub with oil and then salt; cook, uncovered, in moderate oven for about 1 hour or until cooked as desired.

Remove roast from dish; cover. Reserve 2 tablespoons pan juices. Heat reserved juices in same dish, add flour; cook, stirring, until bubbling. Gradually stir in stock, stir until sauce boils and thickens. Strain sauce into jug; serve with roast.

Serves 6 to 8.

■ Best made just before serving.
■ Freeze: Rolls of seasoning suitable.
■ Microwave: Not suitable.

AUSSIE MEAT PIES

1½ cups (225g) plain flour
90g butter, chopped
1 egg
1 tablespoon iced water,
    approximately
2 sheets ready-rolled puff pastry
1 egg, lightly beaten, extra

BEEF FILLING
1 tablespoon vegetable oil
1 medium (150g) onion, chopped
700g minced beef
425g can tomatoes
2 tablespoons tomato paste
¼ cup (60ml) Worcestershire sauce
1 cup (250ml) beef stock
2 tablespoons cornflour
2 tablespoons water

Lightly oil 6 x ½ cup (125ml) pie tins. Process flour and butter until crumbly. Add egg and enough water to make ingredients just cling together; knead dough on floured surface until smooth. Roll into a ball; cover with plastic wrap, refrigerate 30 minutes.

Make 6 tops for pies; turn a pie tin upside down on puff pastry, cut around tin. Repeat to make 6 puff pastry tops; cover and refrigerate until required. Wrap remaining pastry scraps in plastic and refrigerate; use to decorate pies.

Divide dough into 6 portions. Roll each portion between sheets of baking paper until large enough to line prepared tins. Lift pastry into tins, ease into sides, trim edges. Lightly prick bases with fork; refrigerate 30 minutes. Place pastry cases on oven trays, bake blind in moderately hot oven about 20 minutes or until browned lightly; cool.

Spoon cooled filling into pastry cases, brushing edges with a little extra egg; top with puff pastry lids, gently press edges to seal. Decorate with pastry scraps, if desired. Brush pies with a little more extra egg; bake in moderately hot oven about 20 minutes or until browned.

Beef Filling: Heat oil in pan, add onion; cook, stirring until soft. Add mince; cook, stirring, until browned. Add undrained crushed tomatoes, paste, sauce and stock; simmer, uncovered, 20 minutes. Stir in blended cornflour and water, stir over heat until mixture boils and thickens; cool.

Makes 6.

■ Beef filling can be made a day ahead.
■ Storage: Covered, in refrigerator.
■ Freeze: Uncooked pies suitable.
■ Microwave: Not suitable.

Plates, gravy boat and glasses from Waterford Wedgwood

OPPOSITE: Roast Beef with Fresh Herb Seasoning.
RIGHT: Aussie Meat Pies.

China from Waterford Wedgwood

PEPPERED BEEF POT ROAST

2 tablespoons olive oil
2kg whole piece beef rump roast
3 medium (360g) carrots, halved
3 medium (375g) parsnips, halved
1 large (200g) onion, sliced
6 cloves garlic, peeled
3/4 cup (180ml) dry red wine
3/4 cup (180ml) port
3 sprigs fresh rosemary
1 1/2 tablespoons cracked black peppercorns

Heat oil in large pan, add roast; cook until browned all over. Remove from pan. Add carrots, parsnips, onion and garlic to same pan; cook, stirring, until onion is soft. Return roast and any juices to pan with remaining ingredients; simmer, covered, about 45 minutes or until roast is tender. Remove roast from pan; cover to keep warm. Simmer sauce in pan about 5 minutes or until sauce thickens slightly. Serve sauce and vegetables with roast.

Serves 6.

■ Best made just before serving.
■ Freeze: Not suitable.
■ Microwave: Not suitable.

BEEF RISOTTO

Beef rib-eye, boneless sirloin and eye fillet are also suitable for this recipe.

1 tablespoon olive oil
500g beef rump steak, thinly sliced
60g butter
1 medium (150g) onion, chopped
2 cloves garlic, chopped
125g button mushrooms
1 medium (200g) red capsicum, chopped
1 medium (200g) green capsicum, chopped
125g yellow squash, quartered
1 cup (200g) long-grain rice
1 1/2 cups (375ml) beef stock
400g can tomatoes
2 tablespoons tomato paste
1/2 cup (40g) finely grated parmesan cheese
1 tablespoon chopped fresh oregano leaves

Heat oil in pan; cook steak, in batches, until browned. Remove from pan. Melt butter in same pan, add onion and garlic; cook, stirring until onion is soft. Add mushrooms, capsicums and squash; cook, stirring, about 5 minutes or until vegetables are soft. Add rice, stock, undrained crushed tomatoes and paste; simmer, covered, 15 minutes, stirring occasionally, until almost all liquid is absorbed. Return the steak to pan, cover; simmer until rice is tender. Stir in parmesan and oregano.

Serves 4.

■ Best made just before serving.
■ Freeze: Not suitable.
■ Microwave: Not suitable.

BEEF JERKY

Liquid Smoke is a seasoning which gives a delicious wood-fire flavour to beef, chicken or turkey.

750g beef skirt steak, thinly sliced
1/3 cup (80ml) Liquid Smoke
1 teaspoon cooking salt
1 teaspoon cracked black
**   peppercorns**

Combine beef slices and Liquid Smoke in medium bowl; cover and refrigerate 3 hours or overnight.

Place steak in single layer on wire racks over oven trays; sprinkle with half the combined salt and pepper. Turn oven to lowest possible heat (this should be around 100°C). Bake about 3 hours or until steak is dry, turning once during cooking time, sprinkling with remaining salt and pepper mixture.

Serves: 6 to 8.

■ Can be made up to 1 week ahead.
■ Storage: Covered, in refrigerator.
■ Freeze: Not suitable.
■ Microwave: Not suitable.

OPPOSITE: Peppered Beef Pot Roast.
ABOVE: Beef Risotto.
RIGHT: Beef Jerky.

Plate and cutlery from David Jones, Chatswood; glasses from Shack; mats from Kitchen Kapers; napkins from Accoutrement

TRADITIONAL BEEF POT ROAST

1 tablespoon olive oil
125g butter
2kg corner piece beef topside roast
4 medium (680g) carrots, chopped
2 large (600g) potatoes, chopped
1 large (200g) onion, sliced
3 medium (375g) parsnips, chopped
1/4 cup (35g) plain flour
1 litre (4 cups) beef stock
1/2 cup (125ml) dry red wine
1/4 cup (60ml) tomato paste
1/4 cup (60ml) Worcestershire sauce

Heat oil and 20g of the butter in large pan, add roast; cook until browned all over. Remove from pan. Melt another 20g of the butter in same pan; add carrots, potato, onion and parsnips. Cook, stirring until vegetables are just soft and browned lightly; remove from pan. Heat remaining butter in same pan, add flour; cook, stirring, until browned lightly. Remove pan from heat, gradually stir in stock and wine; stir over heat until sauce boils and thickens. Return roast and any juices to pan; add paste and sauce. Simmer, covered, about 2 hours or until roast is tender, turning occasionally. Return vegetables to pan; simmer, uncovered, 20 minutes or until sauce thickens slightly.

Serves 6 to 8.
■ Best made just before serving.
■ Freeze: Not suitable.
■ Microwave: Not suitable.

BEEF IN RED WINE WITH POLENTA

Beef round steak, skirt steak and gravy beef are also suitable for this recipe. Gravy beef is also known as boneless shin.

1/3 cup olive oil
1.5kg beef chuck steak
10 baby (250g) onions
3 cloves garlic, peeled, thinly sliced
1/4 cup (35g) plain flour
2 cups (500ml) dry red wine
1 cup (250ml) beef stock
400g can tomatoes
2 bay leaves
1 tablespoon brown sugar
1/2 cup (40g) grated parmesan cheese
1/2 teaspoon sweet paprika

POLENTA
2 cups (500ml) water
2 cups (500ml) beef stock
1 cup (170g) polenta
40g butter

Heat half the oil in 10 cup (2.5 litre) flameproof casserole dish; cook steak, in batches, stirring, until browned. Remove from dish. Add onions and garlic to same dish; cook, stirring, until onions are browned lightly. Add flour, cook, stirring, 2 minutes, then add wine, stock, undrained crushed tomatoes, bay leaves and sugar. Return steak and any juices to dish; bake, covered, in moderate oven for about 1 1/2 hours or until steak is tender.

Place overlapping polenta rounds on steak mixture and brush with remaining oil. Sprinkle with parmesan and paprika then bake in moderately hot oven for about 20 minutes or until polenta is browned lightly.

Polenta: Bring combined water and stock to boil in medium pan, gradually stir in polenta. Simmer, stirring, about 10 minutes or until mixture is soft and thick. Stir in butter then spread into oiled 26cm x 32cm Swiss roll pan. Cover; refrigerate about 2 hours or until firm. Cut polenta into 5cm rounds.

Serves 6 to 8.
■ Can be prepared a day ahead.
■ Storage: Covered, in refrigerator.
■ Freeze: Steak mixture suitable.
■ Microwave: Not suitable.

ABOVE: Traditional Beef Pot Roast.
OPPOSITE: Beef in Red Wine with Polenta.

BEEF STROGANOFF

We used a whole piece of beef fillet from the rump in this recipe. This is also known as butt fillet.

750g whole piece beef fillet
¼ cup (60ml) vegetable oil
2 medium (300g) onions,
    finely sliced
2 cloves garlic, crushed
2 teaspoons sweet paprika
400g button mushrooms, sliced
⅓ cup (80ml) tomato paste
¼ cup (60ml) dry red wine
1 tablespoon lemon juice
300g sour cream
½ cup milk
¼ cup chopped fresh chives

Cut fillet into thin strips. Heat 2 tablespoons of the oil in medium pan; cook fillet strips, in batches, until browned then remove from pan and keep warm. Heat remaining oil in same pan, add onions and garlic; cook, stirring, until onions are soft. Add paprika and mushrooms; cook, stirring, 2 minutes. Return beef to pan with paste, wine, juice, cream, milk and chives; stir, without boiling, until heated through.

Serves 4 to 6.

■ Best made just before serving.
■ Freeze: Not suitable.
■ Microwave: Not suitable.

BEEF ROULADE

750g minced beef
1 egg, lightly beaten
40g packet French onion soup mix
250g packet frozen spinach, thawed
125g cherry tomatoes
100g mozzarella cheese, chopped

Combine mince, egg and soup mix in medium bowl; mix well. Shape mince mixture into 25cm square on large sheet of greased foil. Squeeze excess moisture from spinach. Place spinach along centre of mince mixture, place tomatoes and mozzarella on either side. Use foil to roll mince then discard. Place roll, seam-side down, on oiled Swiss roll pan; seal ends. Bake in moderately hot oven about 40 minutes or until firm. Cover Roulade, stand 10 minutes before slicing.

Serves 4 to 6.

■ Can be made a day ahead.
■ Storage: Covered, in refrigerator.
■ Freeze: Not suitable.
■ Microwave: Not suitable.

BEEF CURRY WITH COCONUT AND ALMONDS

Round steak, skirt steak and gravy beef are also suitable for this recipe. Gravy beef is also known as boneless shin.

2kg beef chuck steak
1/4 cup (60ml) vegetable oil
2 large (400g) onions, sliced
4 cloves garlic, crushed
3 small fresh red chillies, chopped
1 teaspoon ground turmeric
2 teaspoons ground coriander
1 teaspoon garam marsala
1/2 teaspoon ground black pepper
4 cardamom pods, bruised
2 teaspoons ground ginger
1 star anise
8 curry leaves
400ml can coconut milk
1 cup (250ml) beef stock
3/4 cup (90g) ground almonds

Cut steak into 3cm cubes. Heat oil in pan; cook steak, in batches, until well browned; remove from pan. Add onions and garlic to same pan; cook, stirring, until onions are soft. Add chillies and spices; cook, stirring, until fragrant. Return steak to pan with curry leaves, coconut milk and stock, simmer, covered 1 1/2 hours or until steak is tender. Then simmer, uncovered, another 30 minutes or until sauce thickens; stir in nuts.

Serves 6 to 8.

■ Best made a day ahead.
■ Storage: Covered, in refrigerator.
■ Freeze: Suitable.
■ Microwave: Not suitable.

OPPOSITE TOP: Beef Stroganoff.
OPPOSITE BELOW: Beef Roulade.
RIGHT: Beef Curry with Coconut and Almonds.

Bowls, napkins, pestle and mortar from Accoutrement

COUNTRY-STYLE CASSEROLE WITH DUMPLINGS

Beef chuck steak, skirt steak and gravy beef are also suitable for this recipe. Gravy beef is also known as boneless shin.

1.5kg beef round steak
2 tablespoons olive oil
4 small (320g) onions, quartered
2 cloves garlic, crushed
2 medium (700g) leeks, sliced
2 x 425g cans tomatoes
1/4 cup (60ml) tomato paste
1/2 cup (125ml) dry red wine
1½ cups (375ml) beef stock
500g baby new potatoes, halved
1 bunch (400g) baby carrots
200g green beans, halved

DUMPLINGS
1 cup (150g) self-raising flour
50g butter
1/2 cup (60g) grated tasty cheddar cheese
2 tablespoons chopped fresh parsley
1 egg, lightly beaten
1/3 cup (80ml) milk, approximately

Cut steak into 3cm cubes. Heat half the oil in pan; cook beef, in batches, until well browned; remove from pan. Heat remaining oil in same pan, add onions, garlic and leeks; cook, stirring, until onions are soft and browned lightly.

Return steak and any juices to pan with undrained crushed tomatoes, paste, wine and stock. Simmer, covered, about 1½ hours or until steak is tender, stirring occasionally.

Add potatoes, carrots and beans; simmer, covered, about 10 minutes or until potatoes are tender. Drop tablespoons of dumpling mixture, about 2cm apart, onto hot beef mixture. Simmer, covered, about 15 minutes or until Dumplings are cooked through.

Dumplings: Sift flour into medium bowl, rub in butter, stir in cheddar, parsley, egg and enough milk to mix to a soft, sticky dough.

Serves 6 to 8.

- Country-Style Casserole can be made a day ahead. Dumplings best made just before serving.
- Storage: Casserole, covered, in refrigerator.
- Freeze: Casserole suitable.
- Microwave: Not suitable.

BEEF AND MUSHROOM PIES

6 sheets ready-rolled puff pastry
1 egg, lightly beaten

BEEF FILLING
1 tablespoon olive oil
1 medium (150g) onion, chopped
2 cloves garlic, crushed
200g button mushrooms, thinly sliced
500g minced beef
1 cup (70g) stale breadcrumbs
2 small bacon stock cubes
1/4 cup (60ml) water
1 egg, lightly beaten
1 tablespoon barbecue sauce

Cut a 12cm and a 14cm round from each pastry sheet. Place the 12cm rounds onto oiled oven trays, top with filling, leaving 1cm border. Brush border with egg, top with 14cm rounds of pastry; press edges together with fork. Brush over tops with egg.

Using a sharp knife, make shallow cuts on pastry; bake in hot oven about 20 minutes or until browned.

Beef Filling: Heat oil in large pan, add onion and garlic; cook, stirring, until onion is soft. Add mushrooms; cook, stirring, 2 minutes. Transfer to large bowl then stir in mince, breadcrumbs, crumbled stock cubes, water, egg and sauce. Refrigerate until required.

Makes 6.

- Can be prepared a day ahead.
- Storage: Covered, in refrigerator.
- Freeze: Uncooked filling suitable.
- Microwave: Not suitable.

OPPOSITE: Country-Style Casserole with Dumplings.
ABOVE: Beef and Mushroom Pies.

SWEET AND SOUR MEATBALLS

1kg minced beef
1 medium (150g) onion,
    finely chopped
3 cloves garlic, crushed
1 tablespoon grated fresh ginger
2 teaspoons red curry paste
1/3 cup (25g) stale breadcrumbs
plain flour
vegetable oil, for deep-frying

SWEET AND SOUR SAUCE
850g can pineapple pieces in
    heavy syrup
1 tablespoon peanut oil
1 medium (150g) onion, chopped
1 tablespoon thinly sliced
    fresh ginger
1/2 cup (125ml) white vinegar
1/3 cup (80ml) tomato sauce
1/3 cup (65g) firmly packed
    brown sugar
2 teaspoons cornflour
1 tablespoon water
1 medium (200g) red capsicum,
    chopped
1 medium (200g) green capsicum,
    chopped

Combine mince, onion, garlic, ginger, curry paste and breadcrumbs in large bowl; mix well. Shape rounded tablespoons of mixture into balls. Toss meatballs in flour; shake off excess. Deep-fry meatballs, in batches, in hot oil until browned and cooked through; drain on absorbent paper. Add to pan of Sweet and Sour Sauce just before serving and reheat.

Sweet and Sour Sauce: Drain pineapple; reserve syrup. Heat oil in medium pan, add onion and ginger; cook, stirring, until onion is browned lightly. Add reserved syrup, vinegar, sauce and sugar; stir over heat, without boiling, until sugar is dissolved. Stir in blended cornflour and water; cook, stirring, until sauce boils and thickens. Stir in capsicums and pineapple pieces; simmer, uncovered, 2 minutes or until capsicums are just tender.

Serves 4 to 6.

- Can be made a day ahead.
- Storage: Covered, separately, in refrigerator.
- Freeze: Cooked Meatballs suitable.
- Microwave: Sauce suitable.

BEEF CASSEROLE WITH ROSEMARY

Beef round steak, skirt steak and gravy beef are also suitable for this recipe.

2kg beef chuck steak
2 tablespoons vegetable oil
2 large (400g) onions, chopped
2 cloves garlic, crushed
2 cups (500ml) beef stock
2 sprigs fresh rosemary

Cut steak into 4cm cubes. Heat oil in large pan; cook steak, in batches, stirring, until browned. Remove from pan.

Add onions to same pan; cook, stirring, until onions are soft. Add garlic; cook, stirring, until soft. Return steak and any juices to pan with stock and rosemary. Simmer, covered, 1½ hours; then simmer, uncovered, about 45 minutes or until steak is tender and sauce thickens. Discard rosemary before serving.

Serves: 6 to 8.

- Can be made a day ahead.
- Storage: Covered, in refrigerator.
- Freeze: Suitable.
- Microwave: Not suitable.

PLUM AND PORT MEATLOAF

1kg minced beef
40g packet French onion soup mix
¼ cup (60ml) plum sauce
1½ cups (100g) stale breadcrumbs
2 cloves garlic, crushed
1 egg, lightly beaten
¼ cup (60ml) port
1 tablespoon chopped fresh rosemary leaves
6 green onions, chopped

Oil 14cm x 21cm loaf pan. Combine all ingredients in medium bowl; press into prepared pan, smooth surface. Bake, uncovered, in moderate oven about 1¼ hours or until firm. Turn meatloaf from pan; drain on absorbent paper.

Serves 6.

- Can be made a day ahead.
- Storage: Covered, in refrigerator.
- Freeze: Suitable.
- Microwave: Not suitable.

OPPOSITE TOP: Sweet and Sour Meatballs.
OPPOSITE BELOW: Beef Casserole with Rosemary.
ABOVE: Plum and Port Meatloaf.

ROAST VEAL WITH GREEN PEPPERCORN SAUCE

Order a nut of veal in advance from your butcher and ask that it be tied securely.

1.2kg nut of veal
1 tablespoon olive oil
1 clove garlic, crushed
1 tablespoon plain flour
1⅓ cups (330ml) chicken stock
2 teaspoons Dijon mustard
⅓ cup (80ml) cream
3 teaspoons drained green peppercorns, bruised

Place veal in oiled baking dish; drizzle with oil. Bake, uncovered, in moderately hot oven about 1 hour or until cooked as desired.

Remove veal from pan, cover, stand 10 minutes before slicing thinly. Add garlic to pan juices; stir over heat until garlic is soft. Add flour to pan; cook, stirring, until bubbling. Gradually stir in stock and mustard; stir over heat until mixture boils and thickens. Stir in cream and peppercorns; simmer, uncovered, until heated through. Serve sauce poured over veal.

Serves 6.

■ Best made just before serving.
■ Freeze: Not suitable.
■ Microwave: Not suitable.

THAI BEEF SALAD

Beef rib-eye steak is also known as Scotch fillet.

1 bunch (250g) asparagus, chopped
200g snow peas, halved
100g bean thread noodles
1 medium (170g) Lebanese cucumber
1 medium (120g) carrot
2 cups (160g) mung bean sprouts
1 medium (200g) red capsicum, thinly sliced
4 green onions, chopped
2 tablespoons chopped fresh mint leaves
2 tablespoons chopped fresh coriander leaves
4 (750g) beef rib-eye steaks
⅓ cup (50g) unsalted roasted peanuts
¼ cup fresh coriander leaves

DRESSING
⅓ cup (80ml) mild sweet chilli sauce
2 tablespoons lime juice
2 tablespoons peanut oil
2 teaspoons fish sauce
1 clove garlic, crushed

Place asparagus and snow peas in medium bowl, cover with boiling water, stand 1 minute, drain. Rinse under cold water; drain well. Place noodles in medium bowl, cover with boiling water, stand for 5 minutes; drain. Rinse under cold water; drain well.

Cut cucumber in half lengthways, scoop out seeds; slice thinly. Using a vegetable peeler, first peel then cut carrot into thin strips.

Toss asparagus, snow peas, noodles, cucumber, carrot, bean sprouts, capsicum, onions, chopped herbs and Thai Dressing together in large bowl.

Meanwhile, cook steaks in heated oiled griddle pan (or grill or barbecue) until browned both sides and cooked as desired. Stand beef 10 minutes; slice thinly. Toss slices through salad, top with nuts and coriander leaves.

Dressing: Combine all ingredients in jar; shake well.

Serves 6.

■ Thai Beef Salad best made just before serving. Dressing can be made 2 days ahead.
■ Storage: Dressing, in refrigerator.
■ Freeze: Not suitable.
■ Microwave: Not suitable.

OPPOSITE: Thai Beef Salad.
ABOVE: Roast Veal with Green Peppercorn Sauce.

SEASONED ROAST BREAST OF VEAL

1 bunch (500g) English spinach
1.4kg boned breast of veal
200g sliced pancetta
1/4 cup (35g) pistachio nuts, toasted, chopped
2 teaspoons chopped fresh marjoram leaves
2 teaspoons chopped fresh thyme leaves
2 tablespoons olive oil
2 cloves garlic, crushed
12 medium (900g) egg tomatoes, peeled, quartered
2 tablespoons tomato paste
1 cup (250ml) beef stock
2 teaspoons sugar
2 tablespoons balsamic vinegar

Boil, steam or microwave spinach until just wilted; drain, rinse under cold water; drain. Spread spinach on absorbent paper; press out excess liquid.

Place breast, cut side up, on board. Place spinach, then pancetta, over veal. Sprinkle with pistachios and herbs. Roll breast tightly; secure with string at 2cm intervals.

Heat oil in large flameproof dish, add breast; cook until browned all sides; remove from pan.

Add garlic to dish, cook, stirring, until soft. Add remaining ingredients, bring to boil. Return breast with any juices to dish. Bake, covered, in moderately hot oven, about 1 1/2 hours or until breast is tender. Remove breast from dish, bring tomato mixture to boil; simmer, uncovered, about 15 minutes or until mixture thickens. Return breast to pan, spoon over sauce; simmer, uncovered, until breast is heated through.

Serves 6.

■ Can be made a day ahead.
■ Storage: Covered, in refrigerator.
■ Freeze: Not suitable.
■ Microwave: Not suitable.

VEAL POT ROAST PROVENÇALE

1 tablespoon olive oil
2kg rolled veal shoulder
2 x 400g cans tomatoes
1/2 cup (125ml) dry red wine
1 cup (250ml) beef stock
3 bay leaves
1 tablespoon olive oil, extra
1 medium (350g) leek, sliced
3 cloves garlic, crushed
1 medium (200g) red capsicum, chopped
4 small (520g) zucchini, sliced
2 medium (360g) tomatoes, chopped
2 tablespoons shredded fresh basil leaves

Heat oil in large pan, add shoulder; cook until well browned all over. Add undrained crushed tomatoes, wine, stock and bay leaves; simmer, covered, about 2 hours or until shoulder is tender. Turn shoulder halfway during cooking then simmer, uncovered, about 5 minutes or until sauce thickens.

Meanwhile, heat extra oil in medium pan, add leek, garlic and capsicum; cook, stirring, 2 minutes. Add zucchini and tomatoes; cook, stirring, until vegetables are just tender. Stir in basil. Pour over shoulder, mix through sauce; cook until heated through.

Serves 8.

■ Best made just before serving.
■ Freeze: Not suitable.
■ Microwave: Not suitable.

Plate from Waterford Wedgwood; salt and pepper cruet from The Bay Tree Kitchen Shop; silver tray from Accoutrement

OPPOSITE: Seasoned Roast Breast of Veal.
ABOVE: Veal Pot Roast Provençale.

Plates, cutlery and pot from Bondi Storehouse

BEEF RENDANG

Beef round steak, skirt steak and gravy beef are also suitable for this recipe. Gravy beef is also known as boneless shin.

1kg beef blade steak
2 medium (340g) red onions, chopped
4 cloves garlic, peeled
4 small fresh red chillies
1 tablespoon grated fresh ginger
1 tablespoon chopped fresh lemon grass
1 teaspoon ground turmeric
2 teaspoons ground coriander
400ml can coconut milk
1 cinnamon stick
1 tablespoon tamarind pulp concentrate
8 curry leaves
1 teaspoon sugar

Cut steak into 3cm cubes. Blend or process onions, garlic, chillies, ginger, lemon grass, turmeric and coriander with ⅓ cup (80ml) of the coconut milk until smooth. Combine steak, coconut mixture, remaining coconut milk, cinnamon stick, tamarind and curry leaves in large pan; simmer, uncovered, about 2 hours, stirring occasionally, or until steak is tender. Add sugar; cook, stirring, about 15 minutes or until steak is dark and most of the sauce has evaporated.

Serves 4.

- Best made a day ahead.
- Storage: Covered, in refrigerator.
- Freeze: Suitable.
- Microwave: Not suitable.

VEAL AND VEGETABLE RAGOUT

6 (1.2kg) veal loin chops
plain flour
2 tablespoons olive oil
1 large (200g) onion, chopped
2 cloves garlic, crushed
100g button mushrooms, halved
1 tablespoon plain flour, extra
2 tablespoons tomato paste
½ cup (125ml) dry red wine
3 cups (750ml) beef stock
2 tablespoons Worcestershire sauce
10 (400g) baby new potatoes, halved
1 large (180g) carrot, chopped

Toss chops in flour; shake off excess. Heat half the oil in large pan; cook chops, in batches, until browned both sides. Remove from pan. Heat remaining oil in same pan, add onion, garlic and mushrooms; cook, stirring, until onion is soft. Stir in 1 tablespoon extra flour and paste; cook, stirring, 1 minute. Gradually stir in wine, stock and sauce, bring to boil. Return chops to pan; simmer, covered, 40 minutes or until chops are just tender. Add potatoes; simmer, covered, 10 minutes. Stir in carrot; simmer, uncovered, about 10 minutes or until vegetables are tender.

Serves 6.

- Can be made a day ahead.
- Storage: Covered, in refrigerator.
- Freeze: Suitable.
- Microwave: Not suitable.

OPPOSITE: Veal and Vegetable Ragout.
ABOVE: Beef Rendang.

100

BEEF KORMA

Beef round steak, skirt steak and gravy beef are also suitable for this recipe. Gravy beef is also known as boneless shin.

1kg beef chuck steak
60g ghee
¼ cup (40g) blanched almonds
2 medium (300g) onions, chopped
1 cup (250ml) coconut milk
2 cinnamon sticks
10 cardamom pods, crushed
4 bay leaves
3 cloves
1 tablespoon ground cumin
2 teaspoons ground coriander
1 small fresh red chilli, chopped
1½ tablespoons grated fresh ginger
4 cloves garlic, crushed
½ cup (125ml) yogurt
1 teaspoon salt
½ cup (125ml) water
1 tablespoon tamarind
**   pulp concentrate**

MEATBALLS IN TOMATO SAUCE

1 tablespoon olive oil
1 medium (150g) onion, chopped
2 cloves garlic, crushed
3 (200g) bacon rashers, chopped
¼ cup chopped fresh mint leaves
2 teaspoons chopped fresh
**   rosemary leaves**
1kg minced beef
1 egg, lightly beaten
1 cup (70g) stale breadcrumbs
2 teaspoons grated lemon rind
¼ cup (60ml) olive oil, extra

TOMATO SAUCE
2 tablespoons olive oil
2 medium (300g) onions, chopped
4 cloves garlic, crushed
6 large (1.5kg) tomatoes,
**   peeled, chopped**
¼ cup (60ml) dry red wine
1 teaspoon sugar
2 tablespoons tomato paste

Heat oil in medium pan, add onion, garlic and bacon; cook, stirring until onion is soft. Remove from pan. Combine onion mixture with mint, rosemary, mince, egg, breadcrumbs and rind in large bowl; mix well. Shape ¼ cup mixture into balls. Heat extra oil in same pan; cook meatballs, in batches, until browned all over and cooked as desired. Serve with Tomato Sauce.

Tomato Sauce: Heat oil in pan, add onions and garlic; cook, stirring until onions are soft. Add remaining ingredients; simmer, uncovered, about 1 hour or until mixture thickens.

Serves 4.

■ Can be made a day ahead.
■ Storage: Covered, separately, in refrigerator.
■ Freeze: Cooked meatballs suitable.
■ Microwave: Not suitable.

Glasses from The Pacific East India Company

Cut steak into 3cm cubes. Melt 20g of the ghee in medium pan, add almonds and onions; cook, stirring, until almonds are browned lightly.

Remove from pan; cool. Blend or process onion mixture with coconut milk until smooth.

Melt remaining ghee in same pan, add whole and ground spices, chilli, ginger and garlic; cook, stirring, until fragrant. Add steak, mix well. Add yogurt, 1 tablespoon at a time; cook, stirring well between additions. Stir in onion mixture, salt and water; simmer, covered, 1³/₄ hours. Add tamarind pulp; simmer, uncovered, about 15 minutes, or until steak is tender.

Serves 6.

■ Can be made a day ahead.
■ Storage: Covered, in refrigerator.
■ Freeze: Not suitable.
■ Microwave: Not suitable.

BLANQUETTE D'VEAU

Blanquette d'veau is the French version of veal stew. Imported French dried mixed herbs are sometimes called Herbes de Provence.

1kg veal stewing steak
1 tablespoon olive oil
40g butter
2 large (400g) onions, thinly sliced
2 cloves garlic, crushed
1/4 cup (35g) plain flour
2 teaspoons French mixed herbs
1 cup (250ml) chicken stock
1 cup (250ml) dry white wine
1 tablespoon Dijon mustard
2 large (360g) carrots, roughly
**   chopped**
2 sticks celery, roughly chopped
300g button mushrooms
1/4 cup (60ml) cream
2 tablespoons lemon juice
1 tablespoon chopped fresh parsley

Cut steak into 3cm cubes. Heat oil and butter in large pan, add onions and garlic; cook, stirring, until browned lightly. Add flour to pan; cook, stirring, until bubbling. Add steak and herbs; cook, stirring, until steak is browned lightly. Add stock, wine, mustard, carrots and celery; simmer, covered, 1¹/₂ hours. Add mushrooms; simmer, uncovered, 30 minutes or until steak is tender. Stir in cream and juice. Serve sprinkled with parsley.

Serves 6.

■ Can be made a day ahead.
■ Storage: Covered, in refrigerator.
■ Freeze: Without mushrooms and cream, suitable.
■ Microwave: Not suitable.

OPPOSITE: Meatballs in Tomato Sauce.
LEFT: Beef Korma.
ABOVE: Blanquette D'Veau.

Made in Minutes

Fix some fast family food in the microwave with these delicious time-savers. Beef is a great ingredient to use when cooking in the microwave because of its versatility and moistness. Try combining minced beef with some interesting spices for new twists to old favourites. These are dishes that will keep families – and busy cooks – happy.

MIDDLE EASTERN-STYLE MEATBALLS

1 tablespoon olive oil
1 large (200g) onion, chopped
2 cloves garlic, crushed
2 teaspoons ground ginger
1 teaspoon ground coriander
2 teaspoons ground cumin
1/4 teaspoon ground cinnamon
1/4 teaspoon ground cardamom
1/3 cup (50g) dried currants
2 tablespoons chopped fresh
   coriander leaves
1/3 cup (45g) blanched almonds,
   finely chopped
1kg minced beef
1 tablespoon sambal oelek
1 cup (70g) stale breadcrumbs
1 egg, lightly beaten

YOGURT SAUCE
1½ cups (375ml) yogurt
2 small (260g) Lebanese
   cucumbers, seeded, chopped
1/4 cup chopped fresh mint leaves
2 teaspoons lemon juice

Combine oil, onion, garlic and ground spices in large microwave-safe bowl; cook, covered, on HIGH (100%) for 5 minutes, stirring once during cooking. Add currants, fresh coriander, nuts, mince, sambal oelek, breadcrumbs and egg; mix well. Shape 1/4 cups of mixture into balls. Place meatballs, in single layer, in oiled shallow microwave-safe dish. Cook, uncovered, in 2 batches, on HIGH (100%) 7 minutes, turning once during cooking. Serve meatballs with Yogurt Sauce.

Yogurt Sauce: Combine all ingredients in small bowl.

Serves 4 to 6.

- Can be prepared day ahead.
- Storage: Covered, in refrigerator.
- Freeze: Uncooked meatballs suitable.

Decorative olives, platter, cup and saucer from Sirocco Homewares

BACON AND BEEF LOAF WITH PLUM SAUCE

6 (400g) bacon rashers
500g minced beef
1 small (80g) onion, finely chopped
1 small (70g) carrot, coarsely grated
2 eggs, lightly beaten
1 tablespoon tomato paste
130g can creamed corn
1 cup (70g) stale breadcrumbs
1 tablespoon chopped fresh parsley

PLUM SAUCE
½ cup (125ml) plum sauce
½ cup (125ml) beef stock

Coat a 12cm x 21cm rectangular microwave-safe dish with cooking oil spray, line base and sides with overlapping bacon rashers. Place mince, onion, carrot, eggs, paste, corn, breadcrumbs and parsley in large bowl; mix well. Press mince mixture firmly over bacon. Cook, uncovered, on HIGH (100%) 20 minutes; drain away excess fat halfway through cooking. Serve with Plum Sauce.

Plum Sauce: Combine both ingredients in jug. Cook, uncovered, on HIGH (100%) for 1 minute.

Serves 4 to 6.

■ Can be made a day ahead.
■ Storage: Covered, in refrigerator.
■ Freeze: Suitable.

MEXICAN CHILLI BEEF

1 tablespoon olive oil
1 medium (180g) onion, chopped
2 cloves garlic, crushed
1kg minced beef
1 medium jalapeno pepper, finely chopped
425g can tomatoes
1 cup (250ml) beef stock
¾ cup (180ml) tomato paste
440g can Mexican-style baked beans
2 tablespoons chopped fresh parsley

Combine oil, onion and garlic in large microwave-safe bowl; cook, uncovered, on HIGH (100%) for 4 minutes, stirring once during cooking. Stir in mince; cook, uncovered, on HIGH (100%) 10 minutes, stirring twice during cooking. Add the jalapeno pepper, undrained crushed tomatoes, stock and paste. Cook, uncovered, on HIGH (100%) 30 minutes, stir in undrained beans, cook, uncovered, on HIGH (100%) another 5 minutes. Stir in parsley.

Serves 6.

■ Can be made a day ahead.
■ Storage: Covered, in refrigerator.
■ Freeze: Suitable.

ABOVE: Bacon and Beef Loaf
with Plum Sauce.
OPPOSITE, TOP: Sang Choy Bow.
OPPOSITE, BOTTOM: Mexican Chilli Beef.

SANG CHOY BOW

500g medium uncooked prawns
1 teaspoon sesame oil
1 medium (150g) onion,
    finely chopped
3 cloves garlic, crushed
1 tablespoon grated fresh ginger
1 medium (120g) carrot,
    finely chopped
2 sticks celery, finely chopped
750g minced beef
2 teaspoons sambal oelek
2 teaspoons black bean sauce
1 tablespoon soy sauce
2 tablespoons oyster sauce
2 teaspoons cornflour
2 tablespoons chopped fresh
    coriander leaves
8 lettuce leaves

Shell and devein prawns; process prawns until almost smooth. Combine oil, onion, garlic, ginger, carrot and celery in large microwave-safe bowl; cook, uncovered, on HIGH (100%) 2 minutes, stirring once during cooking. Stir in mince and sambal oelek; cook, uncovered, on HIGH (100%) 8 minutes; stirring once during cooking. Stir in prawns; cook on HIGH (100%) 5 minutes. Stir in blended sauces and cornflour; cook on HIGH (100%) about 5 minutes or until sauce boils and thickens slightly, stirring twice during cooking. Stir in coriander; serve mince mixture in lettuce leaves.

Serves 6 to 8.

■ Best made just before serving.
■ Freeze: Mince mixture suitable.

Tin tray from Accoutrement

Platter and bowls from Accoutrement; serving spoon from Kitchen Kapers

Bowl and platter from Kitchen Kapers

BOLOGNESE SAUCE

1 tablespoon olive oil
1 large (200g) onion, chopped
3 cloves garlic, crushed
3 (200g) bacon rashers, chopped
200g button mushrooms, sliced
1kg minced beef
425g can tomatoes
3/4 cup (180ml) tomato paste
1/2 cup (125ml) dry red wine
1 teaspoon beef stock powder

Combine oil, onion, garlic and bacon in large microwave-safe bowl, cover; cook on HIGH (100%) 6 minutes, stirring once during cooking. Add mushrooms; cook, uncovered, on HIGH (100%) another 4 minutes. Add mince; cook, covered, on HIGH (100%) 10 minutes, stirring twice. Add undrained crushed tomatoes, paste, wine and stock powder; cook, uncovered, on HIGH (100%) 25 minutes or until sauce thickens, stirring 4 times during cooking.

Serves 6.
■ Can be made a day ahead.
■ Storage: Covered, in refrigerator.
■ Freeze: Suitable.

COUNTRY-STYLE BEEF RISSOLES

500g minced beef
1 small (80g) onion, grated
1 clove garlic, crushed
1 tablespoon barbecue sauce
1 tablespoon tomato sauce
1 tablespoon Worcestershire sauce
1 cup (70g) stale breadcrumbs
1 egg, lightly beaten
1 teaspoon chopped fresh
**   thyme leaves**
2 tablespoons chopped
**   fresh parsley**
1 small (130g) tomato, chopped

GLAZE
1/4 cup (60ml) barbecue sauce
2 teaspoons Worcestershire sauce

Oil 28cm round shallow microwave-safe dish. Combine all ingredients in large bowl; mix well. Shape mixture into 8 patties, about 7cm wide. Place the patties around edge of prepared dish; cover, refrigerate 30 minutes. Brush the patties with Glaze; cook, uncovered, on HIGH (100%) 5 minutes. Drain excess liquid from dish; rotate each patty. Cook, uncovered, on HIGH (100%) 3 minutes. Stand, covered, 5 minutes. Serve Rissoles sprinkled with extra chopped fresh parsley, if desired.

Glaze: Combine sauces in bowl.

Serves 4.
■ Best made just before serving.
■ Freeze: Suitable.

ABOVE: Bolognese Sauce.
OPPOSITE: Country-Style Beef Rissoles.

MINCE AND MACARONI CASSEROLE

250g macaroni
1.5 litres (6 cups) boiling water
50g butter, chopped
2 medium (300g) onions,
    finely chopped
3 cloves garlic, crushed
500g minced beef
1/3 cup (50g) plain flour
2 tablespoons tomato paste
1 teaspoon mild English mustard
3 cups (750ml) milk
1 cup (125g) grated tasty
    cheddar cheese
1 cup (100g) grated
    mozzarella cheese
1/4 cup chopped fresh
    flat-leaf parsley

BEEF AND VEGETABLE CURRY

1 medium (150g) onion, chopped
2/3 cup (160ml) mild curry paste
1kg minced beef
425g can tomatoes
1 large (500g) kumara, chopped
1 medium (300g) eggplant, chopped
1 cup (250ml) beef stock
1 cup (125g) frozen peas
1/4 cup chopped fresh
    coriander leaves

Combine onion and paste in large microwave-safe dish; cook, covered, on HIGH (100%) 5 minutes. Add mince; cook, covered, on HIGH (100%) for 10 minutes, stirring twice during cooking. Add undrained crushed tomatoes, kumara, eggplant and stock; cook, uncovered, on HIGH (100%) 20 minutes, stirring twice during cooking. Add peas; cook another 5 minutes. Stir in coriander.

Serves 4 to 6.

■ Can be made a day ahead.
■ Storage: Covered, in refrigerator.
■ Freeze: Suitable.

ABOVE: Beef and Vegetable Curry.
RIGHT: Mince and Macaroni Casserole.
OPPOSITE: Savoury Mince with Fresh Herbs.

Tray, casserole and cutlery from Kitchen Kapers

Spread macaroni over base of large deep microwave-safe dish, cover with boiling water; cook, uncovered, on HIGH (100%) 10 minutes or until just tender, stirring twice during cooking. Drain macaroni, cover to keep warm.

Combine butter, onions and garlic in same dish; cook on HIGH (100%) for 5 minutes. Stir in mince; cook on HIGH (100%) 10 minutes, stirring twice during cooking. Stir in flour, tomato paste and mustard; cook on HIGH (100%) for 2 minutes. Stir in milk; cook on HIGH (100%) 7 minutes, stirring twice during cooking. Stir in macaroni and half the combined cheeses and parsley. Top with remaining cheese and parsley mixture; cook on HIGH (100%) about 2 minutes or until cheese melts.

Serves 4 to 6.

■ Best made just before serving.
■ Freeze: Suitable.

Platter, bowl and spoon from Kitchen Kapers

SAVOURY MINCE WITH FRESH HERBS

1 tablespoon olive oil
2 medium (300g) onions, chopped
1 large (180g) carrot, chopped
3 cloves garlic, crushed
1kg minced beef
4 medium (480g) zucchini, chopped
425g can tomatoes
2/3 cup (160ml) tomato paste
2 tablespoons Worcestershire sauce
1 tablespoon beef stock powder
2 tablespoons sweet fruit chutney
1/4 cup chopped fresh oregano leaves
2 tablespoons chopped fresh basil leaves
1 tablespoon chopped fresh parsley
1 cup (125g) frozen peas, thawed

Combine oil, onions, carrot and garlic in large microwave-safe dish; cook, covered, on HIGH (100%) for 10 minutes, stirring once during cooking.

Stir in mince; cook, covered, on HIGH (100%) 7 minutes, stirring once.

Add zucchini, undrained crushed tomatoes, paste, sauce, stock powder, chutney and herbs; cook, covered, on HIGH (100%) for 15 minutes, stirring every 5 minutes. Stir in peas, cook another 5 minutes.

Serves 6.

■ Can be made a day ahead.
■ Storage: Covered, in refrigerator.
■ Freeze: Suitable.

Sauces, Toppings & Butters

Use these delicious recipes to dress up your barbecued, grilled or pan-fried steaks or veal cutlets. Our range of sauces, toppings and butters has something to suit all tastes, from herb and tomato-based mixtures to creamy concoctions and tangy salsas.

CREAMY GARLIC AND MUSHROOM SAUCE

20g butter
3 cloves garlic, crushed
500g button mushrooms, sliced
½ cup (125ml) chicken stock
1¼ cups (300ml) cream
1 tablespoon grated lemon rind
2 tablespoons chopped fresh chives

Melt butter in medium pan, add garlic; cook until soft. Add mushrooms; cook, stirring, about 5 minutes or until mushrooms are soft. Stir in stock, cream and rind, simmer, uncovered, for about 15 minutes or until sauce thickens slightly. Stir in chives.

Makes about 2 cups (500ml).

■ Sauce can be made a day ahead.
■ Storage: Covered, in refrigerator.
■ Freeze: Not suitable.
■ Microwave: Not suitable.

HONEY CHILLI SAUCE

2 teaspoons peanut oil
2 teaspoons grated fresh ginger
1 clove garlic, crushed
2 small fresh red chillies, chopped
½ cup (125ml) sweet chilli sauce
¼ cup (60ml) honey
2 tablespoons lime juice
¼ cup (60ml) water

Heat oil in small pan, add ginger, garlic and chillies; cook, stirring, until garlic is soft. Add remaining ingredients then simmer about 5 minutes or until sauce thickens slightly; strain.

Makes about 1¼ cups (310ml).

■ Can be made 3 days ahead.
■ Storage: Covered, in refrigerator.
■ Freeze: Suitable.
■ Microwave: Not suitable.

CURRY COCONUT SAUCE

40g butter
2 green onions, sliced
1 tablespoon finely chopped lemon grass
1 tablespoon mild curry powder
400ml can coconut cream
1 tablespoon chopped fresh coriander leaves

Melt butter in small pan, add onions and lemon grass; cook, stirring, until lemon grass is soft. Add curry powder; cook, stirring, until fragrant, then stir in coconut cream; simmer, stirring, until mixture thickens. Stir in coriander.

Makes about 2 cups (500ml).

■ Best made just before serving.
■ Freeze: Not suitable.
■ Microwave: Not suitable.

Honey Chilli Sauce　　Blue Vein Cheese Sauce　　Chilli and Tomato Sauce　　Port and Rosemary Sauce　　Red Wine Mus...

HORSERADISH CREAM SAUCE

1¼ cups (300ml) sour cream
175g horseradish cream
2 tablespoons white wine vinegar
½ cup (125ml) olive oil

Blend or process all ingredients until smooth and creamy.

Makes about 2½ cups (625ml).

■ Can be made 3 days ahead.
■ Storage: Covered, in refrigerator.
■ Freeze: Not suitable.

PORT AND ROSEMARY SAUCE

2 teaspoons vegetable oil
1 medium (150g) onion, chopped
2 cloves garlic, crushed
¼ teaspoon whole black
    peppercorns
1 tablespoon chopped fresh
    rosemary leaves
¾ cup (180ml) port
½ cup (125ml) beef stock
½ cup (125ml) cream
2 teaspoons cornflour
1 tablespoon water
½ teaspoon finely chopped fresh
    rosemary leaves, extra

Heat oil in small pan, add onion, garlic, peppercorns and rosemary; then cook, stirring, until onion is soft. Add port, simmer, uncovered, about 5 minutes or until mixture is reduced to about ⅔ cup (160ml). Stir in stock and cream, then blended cornflour and water; stir until sauce boils and thickens slightly. Strain sauce, stir in extra rosemary.

Makes about 1 cup (250ml).

■ Can be made a day ahead.
■ Storage: Covered, in refrigerator.
■ Freeze: Not suitable.
■ Microwave: Not suitable.

RED WINE AND MUSTARD SAUCE

20g butter
1 small (100g) red onion,
    finely chopped
1 clove garlic, crushed
1½ tablespoons seeded mustard
¾ cup (180ml) beef stock
1 cup (250ml) dry red wine
1 tablespoon tomato paste

Melt butter in medium pan, add onion and garlic; cook, stirring, until onion is soft. Stir in mustard, then stock, wine and paste; simmer, stirring often, about 15 minutes or until mixture is reduced to about 1 cup (250ml). Strain sauce; discard pulp.

Makes about ¾ cup (180ml).

■ Can be made a day ahead.
■ Storage: Covered, in refrigerator.
■ Freeze: Suitable.
■ Microwave: Not suitable.

HOT AND SPICY SAUCE

We used a ready-made pesto sauce flavoured with roasted capsicum in this recipe.

1 tablespoon olive oil
1 large (200g) onion, chopped
4 medium (760g) tomatoes,
    chopped
1 tablespoon balsamic vinegar
1 teaspoon sugar
½ cup (125ml) pesto sauce
2 teaspoons sambal oelek

Heat oil in pan, add onion; cook, stirring until onion is soft. Add remaining ingredients, simmer about 10 minutes or until tomatoes are pulpy.

Makes about 2½ cups (625ml).

■ Can be made 3 days ahead.
■ Storage: Covered, in refrigerator.
■ Freeze: Suitable.
■ Microwave: Not suitable.

CHILLI AND TOMATO SAUCE

1 large (200g) onion, chopped
2 cloves garlic, peeled, chopped
3 small fresh red chillies, chopped
1 teaspoon ground cumin
1 teaspoon ground coriander
1 tablespoon tomato paste
¼ cup (50g) firmly packed
    brown sugar
425g can tomatoes
¼ cup (60ml) white wine vinegar
¼ cup (60ml) Worcestershire sauce
¼ cup (60ml) olive oil

Process onion, garlic, chillies, spices, paste, sugar and undrained crushed tomatoes until smooth. Add vinegar, sauce and oil, process until combined. Transfer the mixture to a medium pan, simmer, uncovered, stirring occasionally, about 15 minutes or until sauce has reduced to about 2 cups (500ml).

Makes about 2 cups (500ml).

■ Can be made a day ahead.
■ Storage: Covered, in refrigerator.
■ Freeze: Suitable.
■ Microwave: Not suitable.

BLUE VEIN CHEESE SAUCE

40g butter
1 clove garlic, crushed
1 small (80g) onion, finely chopped
125g blue vein cheese, chopped
½ cup (125ml) cream
½ cup (125ml) sour cream
1 teaspoon Dijon mustard
1 tablespoon chopped fresh parsley

Melt butter in small pan, add garlic and onion; cook, stirring, until onion is soft. Add blue vein; cook, stirring, until melted. Stir in cream, sour cream and mustard; simmer, stirring, until mixture thickens slightly; stir in parsley.

Makes about 2 cups (500ml).

■ Best made just before serving.
■ Freeze: Not suitable.
■ Microwave: Not suitable.

Horseradish Cream Sauce   *Hot and Spicy Sauce*   *Curry Coconut Sauce*   *Creamy Garlic and Mushroom Sauce*

Satay Sauce

Devilled Sauce

SATAY SAUCE

2 teaspoons peanut oil
1 small (80g) onion, finely chopped
1 clove garlic, crushed
1 teaspoon sambal oelek
1 teaspoon mild curry powder
1 teaspoon ground cumin
2 cups (500ml) water
1 teaspoon chicken stock powder
2 teaspoons soy sauce
1/2 cup (130g) crunchy peanut butter
1 tablespoon lime juice
1/4 cup (60ml) coconut milk
1 tablespoon chopped fresh
  coriander leaves

Heat oil in small pan, add onion, garlic, sambal oelek and spices; cook, stirring, until onion is soft. Add water, stock powder, sauce and peanut butter, simmer, uncovered, about 15 minutes or until sauce thickens. Add remaining ingredients, stir until heated through.

Makes about 2 cups (500ml).

■ Can be made a day ahead.
■ Storage: Covered, in refrigerator.
■ Freeze: Not suitable.
■ Microwave: Not suitable.

DEVILLED SAUCE

1 tablespoon olive oil
1 medium (150g) onion, chopped
2 cloves garlic, crushed
1 teaspoon hot paprika
1/4 cup (50g) firmly packed
  brown sugar
1/3 cup (80ml) cider vinegar
1 tablespoon chopped fresh
  thyme leaves
1 teaspoon Tabasco sauce
1 tablespoon Worcestershire sauce
2 cups (500ml) beef stock
1 tablespoon cornflour
1 tablespoon water

Heat oil in medium pan, add onion and garlic; cook, stirring, until onion is soft. Stir in paprika, then sugar and vinegar; cook, stirring, without boiling, until sugar is dissolved; simmer 2 minutes. Add thyme, sauces and stock, simmer, uncovered, about 15 minutes or until reduced to about 2 cups (500ml). Stir in blended cornflour and water, stir until sauce boils and thickens.

Makes about 2 cups (500ml).

■ Can be made a day ahead.
■ Storage: Covered, in refrigerator.
■ Freeze: Not suitable.
■ Microwave: Not suitable.

AVOCADO WASABI SALSA

1 medium (250g) avocado,
  finely chopped
1 small (150g) red capsicum,
  finely chopped
1 small (150g) green capsicum,
  finely chopped
2 teaspoons wasabi paste
1 tablespoon white wine vinegar
2 tablespoons lemon juice
1 tablespoon olive oil

Place all ingredients in medium bowl; stir gently to combine.

Makes about 2 cups (500ml).

■ Best made just before serving.
■ Freeze: Not suitable.

TOMATO, PEACH AND CORIANDER SALSA

2 large (500g) tomatoes,
  seeded, chopped
1/2 x 425g can peach slices,
  drained, chopped
1 small (80g) onion, finely chopped
1 medium (170g) Lebanese
  cucumber, seeded, chopped
1 tablespoon chopped fresh
  coriander leaves
1 tablespoon sweet chilli sauce
2 tablespoons lime juice
2 tablespoons peanut oil

Place all ingredients in medium bowl; stir gently to combine.

Makes about 3 cups (750ml).

■ Best made just before serving.
■ Freeze: Not suitable.

ASPARAGUS, OLIVE AND BOCCONCINI SALSA

2 bunches (about 360g) thin
  asparagus
3/4 cup (120g) seeded black
  olives, chopped
200g bocconcini cheese,
  finely chopped
2 tablespoons chopped fresh
  mint leaves
1 tablespoon chopped fresh parsley
2 tablespoons olive oil
1 1/2 tablespoons lime juice
1 clove garlic, crushed
1/2 teaspoon sugar

Add asparagus to large pan of boiling water, drain immediately, rinse under cold water, pat dry with absorbent paper; slice asparagus thinly. Combine asparagus with remaining ingredients in medium bowl; mix gently.

Makes about 3 cups (750ml).

■ Best made just before serving.
■ Freeze: Not suitable.
■ Microwave: Asparagus suitable.

Avocado Wasabi Salsa

Tomato, Peach and Coriander Salsa

Asparagus, Olive and Bocconcini Salsa

ROASTED CAPSICUM, OLIVE AND PAPRIKA BUTTER

1 medium (200g) red capsicum
125g butter, softened
¼ cup (30g) seeded black olives, thinly sliced
½ teaspoon sweet paprika

Quarter capsicum, remove seeds and membranes. Roast under grill or in very hot oven, skin side up until skin blisters and blackens. Cover capsicum pieces in plastic or paper for 5 minutes, peel away skin, chop finely.

Beat butter in small bowl with electric mixer until light and creamy, then stir in capsicum, olives and paprika. Cover, refrigerate until firm.

Serves 4 to 6.

■ Butter can be made 3 days ahead.
■ Storage: Covered, in refrigerator.
■ Freeze: Suitable.
■ Microwave: Not suitable.

PESTO BUTTER

125g butter, softened
¼ cup (40g) pine nuts, toasted, chopped
¼ cup (20g) finely grated parmesan cheese
¼ cup (60ml) pesto
½ teaspoon cracked black peppercorns

Beat butter in small bowl with electric mixer until light and creamy, stir in remaining ingredients. Cover tightly, refrigerate until firm.

Serves 4 to 6.

■ Can be made 3 days ahead.
■ Storage: Covered, in refrigerator.
■ Freeze: Suitable.

SUN-DRIED TOMATO AND RED ONION BUTTER

2 teaspoons olive oil
1 small (100g) red onion, finely chopped
1 clove garlic, crushed
125g butter, softened
2 tablespoons drained, chopped sun-dried tomatoes
1 tablespoon chopped fresh parsley
¼ teaspoon ground coriander
1 tablespoon lemon juice

Heat oil in small pan, add onion and garlic; cook, stirring, until onion is soft; cool. Beat butter in small bowl with electric mixer until light and creamy, stir in onion mixture and remaining ingredients. Cover, refrigerate until firm.

Serves 4 to 6.

■ Butter can be made 3 days ahead.
■ Storage: Covered, in refrigerator.
■ Freeze: Suitable.
■ Microwave: Onion mixture suitable.

ANCHOVY BUTTER

125g butter, softened
4 drained anchovy fillets, chopped
2 teaspoons lemon juice
1 tablespoon chopped fresh basil leaves
1 tablespoon finely grated parmesan cheese
1 teaspoon tomato paste

Beat butter in small bowl with electric mixer until light and creamy, beat in remaining ingredients. Cover tightly, refrigerate until firm.

Serves 4 to 6.

■ Can be made 3 days ahead.
■ Storage: Covered, in refrigerator.
■ Freeze: Suitable.

LIME, CHILLI AND CORIANDER BUTTER

125g butter, softened
1 small fresh red chilli, finely chopped
2 tablespoons chopped fresh coriander leaves
2 teaspoons grated lime rind
2 teaspoons lime juice
¼ teaspoon cracked black peppercorns

Beat butter in small bowl with electric mixer until light and creamy, stir in remaining ingredients. Cover, refrigerate until firm.

Serves 4 to 6.

■ Can be made 3 days ahead.
■ Storage: Covered, in refrigerator.
■ Freeze: Suitable.

GREEN PEPPERCORN BUTTER

1 teaspoon olive oil
1 small (80g) onion, finely chopped
1 clove garlic, crushed
125g butter, softened
2 tablespoons canned green peppercorns, rinsed, drained

Heat oil in small pan, add onion and garlic; cook, stirring, until onion is soft; cool. Beat butter in small bowl with electric mixer until light and creamy, stir in onion mixture and peppercorns. Cover, refrigerate until firm.

Serves 4 to 6.

■ Can be made 3 days ahead.
■ Storage: Covered, in refrigerator.
■ Freeze: Suitable.
■ Microwave: Onion mixture suitable.

Anchovy Butter

Roasted Capsicum, Olive and Paprika Butter

Green Peppercorn Butter

Sun-Dried Tomato and Red Onion Butter

Lime, Chilli and Coriander Butter

Pesto Butter

The Brief on Beef

Comprehensive and essential information on all aspects of beef preparation, hygiene, refrigeration and freezing, plus tips on various cooking methods.

Purchasing & storing

■ When shopping, take along an insulated bag for chilled and frozen meat products, making certain these are the last items purchased.

■ Once home, place all chilled and frozen food in your refrigerator or freezer immediately.

■ Allow 125g to 150g (about 5oz) of lean boneless meat per person.

■ Meat should be a bright, clear colour and have a fresh appearance.

■ Select lean meat; whatever fat there is should be a pale cream in colour.

■ Meat should be kept as dry as possible and never sit in its own juice. Cold air should be able to circulate freely around the piece of meat.

■ The more cutting and preparation the meat has been subjected to, the briefer the allowable storage time. This is why storage time for mince (ground meat) is less than for steak or chops.

■ If meat is used within 2 days, it can be left in its original wrapping.

■ Meat that has been kept in the refrigerator for 2 to 3 days will be more tender than meat cooked on day of purchase. This is due to natural enzymes softening the muscle fibre.

■ To maximise freshness, meat should be refrigerated, in a single layer, in a container covered loosely with foil.

Refrigeration time for meat

Mince (ground meat) and sausages	2 days
Diced meat	3 days
Steaks, chops and cutlets	4 days
Roasting joints (with bone in)	3 to 5 days
Roasting joints (boned and rolled)	2 to 3 days
Corned beef	1 week
Vacuum-packed beef	4 weeks

Hygiene

■ Careful attention to hygiene when handling meat is essential. Most cases of food poisoning result from food being unrefrigerated: the longer food stands at room temperature, the greater the chance of food poisoning.

■ Wash hands and utensils thoroughly before and after handling meat.

■ Never handle cooked and uncooked meats together: neither cut them with the same utensils nor on the same board.

■ Store cooked meat above raw meat so there's no chance that juices can drip onto cooked meat.

■ Defrost frozen meat in the refrigerator before cooking; never defrost at room temperature.

■ Refrigerate leftover cooked meat as soon as possible.

Freezer hints

■ Meat should be sealed tightly with plastic wrap to protect it from freezer burn, dehydration and oxidation of fat.

■ Your freezer should be set at -15°C (5°F) or lower.

■ When freezing steak, chops or cutlets, pack individually in plastic wrap then in plastic freezer bags, expelling all air.

■ Defrost frozen meat in the refrigerator or on defrost setting in a microwave oven.

■ Do not thaw meat at room temperature or in hot water.

■ Meat that has been thawed should not be refrozen in its raw state. If it is not to be eaten immediately, it should be cooked first before refrozen safely.

■ Make sure there is plenty of space in the freezer. Cold air needs to circulate freely around food to freeze it quickly.

■ Don't attempt to freeze too much at once; smaller batches freeze far more rapidly.

■ Mince (ground meat) has a greater surface area, so it should be cooked as soon as possible after defrosting.

Preparing meat to be frozen

■ Each package should carry a label showing name of cut, weight or amount and date of packaging.

■ Air should be expelled either by pressing out when wrapping or with the aid of a pump. Twist, then seal bags with a strip of masking tape.

■ Meat purchased on a styrofoam tray should be repacked before freezing, discarding styrofoam tray.

■ Cutting meat into strips or cubes before freezing will save time in meal preparation. Weigh out meal-sized portions and place in plastic bags, filling corners with meat. Make package as flat as possible so meat will defrost quickly when needed. Expel air and seal with tape.

Frozen meat storage times (at -15°C/5°F)

Beef joint *(solid)*	8 months
Beef joint *(rolled)*	6 months
Beef steaks, stew meat	6 months
Veal joints	6 months
Veal steaks, chops	4 months
Lean minced *(ground)* meats	2 months

Stir-fries

- Cut meat into thin strips across the grain. This shortens the fibre, making the pieces more tender.
- Have the wok or pan well heated: searing the meat seals in the juices and makes it cook more quickly. Too low a temperature stews meat in its own juices and toughens it.
- To maintain a consistently high temperature, stir-fry meat in a number of small batches.
- If stir-frying marinated meat, thoroughly drain off the marinade before cooking meat. Return any reserved marinade to wok at the end of cooking time, and bring to a boil just before serving.

Roasts

- Meat can be elevated over a roasting pan, either on a rack or over a bed of vegetables. Using the vegetables also adds flavour to the meat juices that collect in the pan.
- The roast should rest before carving, allowing juices to settle into the meat.
- When carving, slice across the grain. This shortens the fibre, making the slices more tender.

- Weigh meat to be able to accurately calculate cooking time.
- For accuracy, use a meat thermometer. Calculate cooking time then insert the thermometer into the thickest part of the meat at the beginning of the cooking time.

Rare = 60°C/140°F
Medium = 65-70°C/150-160°F
Well done = 75°C/170°F

Pan-fries, barbecues & grills

- Have pan, barbecue or grill well heated to ensure meat is sealed. Meat should sizzle immediately when it touches the base of the pan or barbecue to avoid it stewing and becoming tough.
- When pan-frying and barbecuing, seal meat on both sides. Beads of juice appearing on the uncooked side indicate the meat is ready to turn. If steak is turned too soon or too often, it becomes dry and tough.
- Rare meat needs only to be well sealed. To avoid charring if cooking further, reduce heat after the meat is sealed.
- Do not cut into steak to see if cooked. Press surface with tongs: cooked meat will offer some resistance and spring back. It's important to rest the meat a little after cooking to allow the juices to settle. Cutting the steak too soon will allow juices to escape.
- If using a marinade, those containing honey or other sugary ingredients burn easily so it may be necessary to reduce heat immediately after sealing.

Casseroles & curries

- Seal meat in a preheated pan over high heat in small batches to lock in flavoursome juices and develop colour.
- Once liquid is added, allow the casserole to return to the boil, then immediately reduce heat. Cover and simmer until tender, stirring occasionally to prevent sticking.
- Don't allow a casserole or curry to boil rapidly because doing so will toughen the meat considerably.
- A pressure cooker is a great help in cooking casseroles as it can reduce cooking time by about a third.

Beef stock

3kg beef bones
1 tablespoon vegetable oil
3 medium (360g) carrots, roughly chopped
1 medium (350g) leek, sliced
2 medium (300g) onions, roughly chopped
3 bay leaves
8 black peppercorns
4 fresh parsley sprigs
1 tablespoon fresh thyme sprigs
1 tablespoon fresh oregano sprigs
5 litres (20 cups) water

Place bones on 2 large baking trays; cook, uncovered, in moderate oven about 2 hours or until bones are well browned.

Heat oil in large pan, add vegetables; cook, stirring, about 10 minutes or until vegetables are browned.

Combine bones, vegetables and remaining ingredients in large pan; simmer, uncovered, 4 hours. Skim surface occasionally during cooking. Strain stock; cool. Cover; refrigerate 6 hours or overnight. Remove and discard fat from surface.

Makes about 1.5 litres (6 cups).
- Must be made a day ahead.
- Storage: Covered, in refrigerator.
- Freeze: Suitable.
- Microwave: Not suitable.

Beef roasting chart

Beef cut	Oven temp	Rare 60°C	Medium 65-70°C	Well done 75°C
Fillet	200°C/400°F	15-20min per 500g/1lb	20-25min per 500g/1lb	25-30min per 500g/1lb
All other	180°C/350°F	20-25min per 500g/1lb	25-30min per 500g/1lb	30-35min per 500g/1lb

Beef Strips

Prepared from blade, fillet, rib eye,
round, rump, sirloin, topside

**Master Trim
Round Medallion**

**Master Trim
Rump Medallion**

**Master Trim
Rump Centre Steak**

**Rib Eye Steak
(Scotch Fillet)**

Rib Steak

Rump Steak

Fillet Steak

Diced Beef

Prepared from rump, sirloin,
rib eye, fillet

Blade Steak, boneless

Blade Steak, bone in

Silverside Minute Steak

Chuck Steak

**Gravy Beef
(Shin, boneless)**

**Osso Bucco
(Shin, bone in)**

Brisket

Cuts of Beef

Casserole   Pot Roast   Kettle Barbecue   Stir Fry   Barbecue   Pan Fry   Grill   Oven Roast

Rump Roast

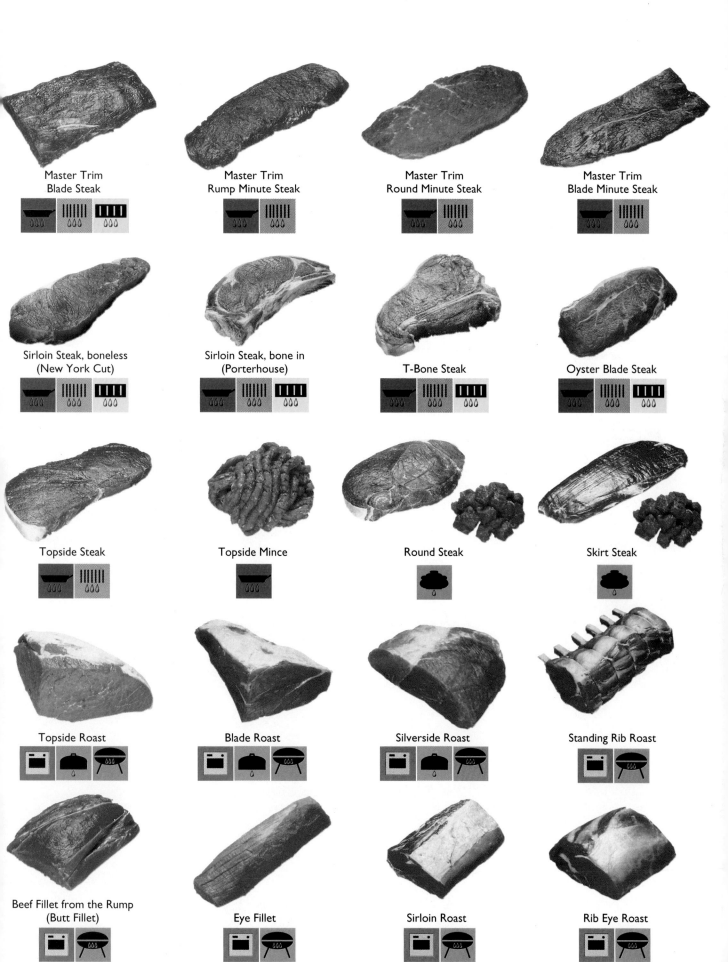

Master Trim
Blade Steak

Master Trim
Rump Minute Steak

Master Trim
Round Minute Steak

Master Trim
Blade Minute Steak

Sirloin Steak, boneless
(New York Cut)

Sirloin Steak, bone in
(Porterhouse)

T-Bone Steak

Oyster Blade Steak

Topside Steak

Topside Mince

Round Steak

Skirt Steak

Topside Roast

Blade Roast

Silverside Roast

Standing Rib Roast

Beef Fillet from the Rump
(Butt Fillet)

Eye Fillet

Sirloin Roast

Rib Eye Roast

119

Glossary

Here are some terms, names and alternatives to help everyone use and understand our recipes perfectly.

Thyme

Coriander

Curry leaves

Tarragon

Bay leaves

Sage

Oregano

Marjoram

Basil

Lebanese cucumber

ALLSPICE: also known as pimento or Jamaican pepper; available whole or ground. Tastes like a blend of cinnamon, clove and nutmeg.

BACON RASHERS: slices of bacon.

BARBECUE SAUCE: a spicy tomato-based sauce used to marinade, baste or as an accompaniment.

BEANS:

Baked, Mexican-style: we used a canned mixture consisting of haricot (navy) beans, tomato puree, peppers, onion and various spices.

Black, salted: fermented, salted and dried soy beans. Soak, drain and rinse dried beans; chop before or mash during cooking to release flavour. **Black Bean Sauce** is made from fermented soy beans, spices, water and wheat flour.

BOK CHOY: also called pak choi or Chinese white cabbage; has a fresh, mild mustard taste and is good braised or in stir-fries. Baby bok choy is also available.

BREADCRUMBS:

Packaged: use fine-textured, crunchy, purchased breadcrumbs.

Stale: use 1- or 2-day-old bread made into crumbs by grating, blending or processing.

BURRITO: a soft flour tortilla, filled then baked and served, with cheese melted over the top, with a sauce.

BUTTER: use salted or unsalted (also called sweet) butter; 125g is equal to 1 stick butter.

BUTTERMILK: made by adding a culture to low-fat milk to give a slightly sour taste; low-fat yogurt can be substituted.

CAPSICUM: bell pepper or, simply, pepper. Seeds and membranes should be discarded before use.

CHEESE:

Blue vein: mould-treated cheese mottled with blue veining; we used a firm, fairly strong-flavoured variety.

Bocconcini: small rounds of fresh "baby" mozzarella, a delicate, semi-soft, white cheese traditionally made in Italy from buffalo milk. Spoils rapidly so must be kept under refrigeration, in brine, for a maximum of 2 days.

Fetta: Greek in origin; a crumbly textured goat- or sheep-milk cheese having a sharp, salty taste.

Haloumi: a firm, cream-coloured sheep-milk cheese matured in brine; somewhat like a minty, salty fetta in flavour.

Mozzarella: a semi-soft cheese with a delicate, fresh taste; has a low melting point and stringy texture when heated.

Parmesan: a sharp-tasting, dry, hard cheese, made from skim or part skim milk and aged for at least a year before being sold. The best quality is Parmigiano Reggiano, from Italy, aged a minimum three years.

Ricotta: a sweet, fairly moist, fresh curd cheese having a low fat content.

Romano: a hard, straw-coloured cheese with a grainy texture

Ground almonds

Almond slivers

Blanched almonds

Baby eggplant

Eggplant

Flat parsley

Curly parsley

Mint

Rosemary

Chives

and sharp, tangy flavour, usually made from a combination of cow and goat or sheep milk. A good grating cheese.

Swiss: generic name for a variety of cheeses originating in Switzerland, among them emmenthaler and gruyere.

Tasty: matured Cheddar; use an aged, hard, pronounced-flavoured variety.

CHICKPEAS: also called garbanzos or channa; an irregularly round, sandy-coloured legume used extensively in Mediterranean and Hispanic cooking.

CHILLIES: available in many different types and sizes. Use rubber gloves when seeding and chopping fresh chillies, as they can burn your skin. Removing seeds and membranes lessens the heat level.

Flakes: crushed dried chillies.

Jalapeños: fairly hot green chillies, available in brine bottled or fresh from specialty greengrocers.

Mexican-style powder: a blend of chilli powder, paprika, oregano, cumin, pepper and garlic.

Powder: the Asian variety is the hottest and is made from ground chillies; it can be used as a substitute for fresh chillies, assuming that 1/2 teaspoon chilli powder is equal to1 medium chopped fresh chilli.

Sweet chilli sauce: a comparatively mild Thai-type commercial sauce made from red chillies, sugar, garlic and vinegar.

CHINESE BARBECUE SAUCE: a thick, sweet and salty commercial sauce used in marinades; made from fermented soy beans, vinegar, garlic, pepper and various spices. Available from Asian specialty stores.

CHINESE CABBAGE: also called Peking cabbage or wong bok; has a tight head of pale-green crinkled leaves. Milder in taste than Western cabbage; good eaten raw or in soups and stir-fries.

CHOY SUM: also called flowering bok choy or flowering white cabbage; has

small yellow flowers which are eaten along with the leaves and stems. Good steamed or stir-fried.

COCONUT:
Cream: available in cans and cartons; made from coconut and water.
Desiccated: unsweetened, concentrated, dried shredded coconut.

CORNFLOUR: cornstarch.

COUSCOUS: a fine, grain-like cereal product, originally from North Africa; made from semolina.

CREAM (minimum fat content 35%): fresh pouring cream.
Sour (minimum fat content 35%): a thick, commercially cultured soured cream.
Thickened (minimum fat content 35%): a whipping cream containing a thickener.

CURRY LEAVES: bright-green, shiny, sharp-ended, fresh green leaves used in cooking Indian curries.

DASHI: the basic fish and seaweed stock that accounts for the distinctive flavour of many Japanese dishes. It is made from dried bonito flakes and kelp (kombu). Instant dashi powder, also known as dashi-no-moto, is a concentrated granulated powder. Available from Asian specialty stores.

EGGPLANT: aubergine.

ENGLISH SPINACH: true spinach (the green vegetable often called spinach is correctly silverbeet). Delicate, crinkled green leaves on thin stems; high in iron; it's good eaten raw in salads or steamed gently on its own.

FISH SAUCE: also called nam pla or nuoc nam; made from pulverised salted fermented fish, most often anchovies. Has a pungent smell and strong taste; use sparingly. There are many kinds, of varying intensity.

FIVE-SPICE POWDER: a fragrant mixture of ground cinnamon, cloves, star-

anise, Szechuan pepper and fennel.

FLOUR:
Plain: all-purpose flour.
Self-raising: substitute with 1 cup (150g) plain (all-purpose) flour and 2 level teaspoons baking powder sifted together several times before using.

FRENCH DRIED MIXED HERBS: consists of parsley flakes, chervil, tarragon leaves and chives; also called Herbes de Provence.

GARAM MASALA: a powdered blend of spices, originally from North India, based on cardamom, cinnamon, cloves, coriander and cumin. Sometimes chilli is added, making a hot variation.

GHEE: clarified butter; with the milk solids removed, this fat can be heated to a high temperature without burning.

GHERKIN: cornichon; young, dark-green cucumbers grown especially for pickling.

GREEN GINGER WINE: alcoholic sweet wine infused with finely ground ginger.

HERBS: when specified, we used dried (not ground) herbs in the proportion of 1 teaspoon dried herbs being equal to 4 teaspoons (1 tablespoon) chopped fresh herbs.

HOISIN SAUCE: a thick, sweet and spicy Chinese paste made from salted, fermented soy beans, onions and garlic; used as a marinade or baste, or to accent stir-fries and barbecued or roasted foods.

HORSERADISH CREAM: a creamy paste of grated horseradish, vinegar, oil and sugar.

HUMMUS: a Middle-Eastern dip made of chickpeas, tahini, garlic and lemon juice.

INDIRECT METHOD: a kettle barbecue cooking method where the heat beads or coals are placed

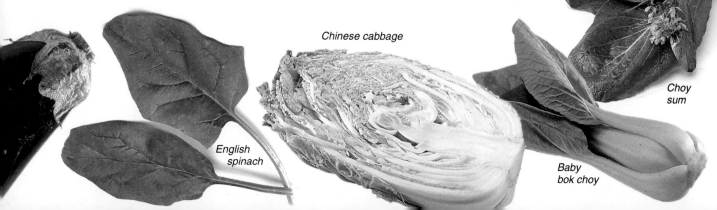

Chinese cabbage

English spinach

Choy sum

Baby bok choy

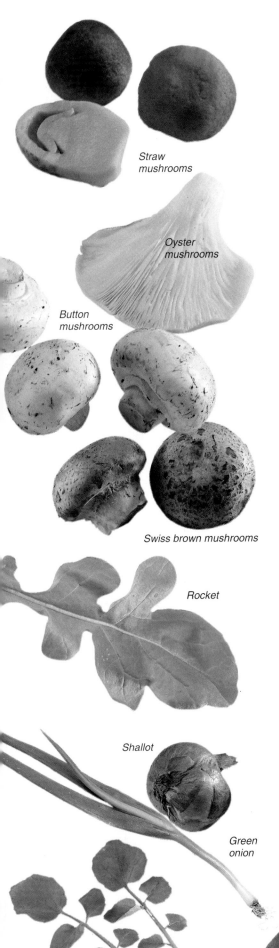

Straw mushrooms

Oyster mushrooms

Button mushrooms

Swiss brown mushrooms

Rocket

Shallot

Green onion

Watercress

around the outside perimeter of the bottom grill, surrounding the food rather than burning directly under it.

KAFFIR LIME LEAVES: Originally grown in South Africa and Southeast Asia; leaves of a small citrus tree bearing a bumpy, wrinkled-skinned, pear-shaped yellow-green fruit. Used fresh or dried in many Asian dishes.

KUMARA: an orange-coloured sweet potato, often incorrectly called a yam.

LEMON GRASS: a tall, clumping, lemon-smelling and tasting, sharp-edged grass; the white lower part of each stem is chopped and used in Asian cooking.

LIQUID SMOKE: we used Tone's Hickory Barbecue Flavour liquid smoke as a seasoning; made of water, natural smoke flavour, molasses and vinegar. Available from barbecue outlets.

MARSALA: a sweet fortified wine originating in Sicily.

MIRIN: a sweet, low-alcohol rice wine used in Japanese cooking.

MIXED BABY LETTUCE LEAVES: also known as mesclun, salad mix or gourmet salad mix; a mixture of assorted young lettuce and other green leaves.

NOODLES:

Bean thread: also called cellophane; made from green mung bean flour. Good softened in soups and salads or deep-fried with vegetables.

Fresh rice: thick, wide, almost white in colour; made from rice and vegetable oil. Must be covered with boiling water to remove starch and excess oil before using in soups and stir-fries.

Hokkien: a fresh egg and wheat flour noodle; looks like a thicker, yellow-brown spaghetti. Sometimes referred to as stir-fry noodles and best in fast-fried dishes.

Rice vermicelli: also called rice stick; made from rice flour. Must be soaked before using in stir-fries or soups.

OIL:

Chilli: made by steeping red chillies in vegetable oil; intensely hot in flavour.

Cooking oil spray: vegetable oil in an aerosol can, available in supermarkets.

Olive: a mono-unsaturated oil, made from the pressing of tree-ripened olives; especially good for everyday cooking.

Peanut: pressed from ground peanuts, is the most commonly used oil in Asian cooking because of its high smoke point.

Sesame: an oil much used in Asian cooking; made from roasted, crushed white sesame seeds, it's used as a flavouring rather than a cooking medium.

Vegetable: any of a wide number of cooking oils having a plant rather than an animal source.

ONION:

Green: also known as scallion or (incorrectly) as shallot; an immature onion picked before the bulb has formed, having a long, bright-green edible stalk.

Red: also known as Spanish, red Spanish or Bermuda onion; a sweet-flavoured, large, purple-red onion that is particularly good eaten raw in salads.

OYSTER SAUCE: Asian in origin, this rich, brown sauce is made from oysters and brine, cooked with salt and soy sauce then thickened with starches.

PANCETTA: an Italian salt-cured pork roll, usually cut from the belly; used, diced, in many meat dishes to add flavour. Bacon can be substituted.

PAPRIKA: ground dried red capsicum (bell pepper); available sweet or hot.

PLUM SAUCE: a thick, sweet and sour dipping sauce made from plums, vinegar, sugar, chillies and spices.

POLENTA: a flour-like cereal made from ground corn (maize); similar to cornmeal but coarser and darker in colour; also the name for the cooked dish made from it.

PRAWNS: shrimp.

PROSCIUTTO: salt-cured, air-dried (unsmoked) pressed ham; usually sold in paper-thin slices, ready to eat.

RAISINS: dried sweet grapes.

RICE WINE: a sweet, gold-coloured, low-alcohol wine made from fermented steamed rice.

ROCKET: also called arugula, rugula or rucola; a peppery-tasting salad green.

SAMBAL OELEK (also ulek or olek): Indonesian in origin; a salty paste made from ground chillies, sugar and spices.

SEASONED PEPPER: a combination of ground black pepper, sugar and powdered capsicum (bell pepper).

Kumara

Lemon grass

SHALLOTS: also called French shallots, golden shallots or eshalots; small, elongated, brown-skinned members of the onion family. Grows in tight clusters similar to garlic.

SMOKING CHIPS: small pieces of various wood chips packaged and available from barbecue outlets; we used Hickory Wood Chunks.

SNOW PEAS: also called mange tout ("eat all").

SOY SAUCE: made from fermented soy beans. Several variations are available in most supermarkets and Asian food stores, among them are salt-reduced, light, sweet and salty.

STAR ANISE: a dried star-shaped pod from an Asian evergreen tree; the seeds have a stringent aniseed flavour.

SUET: the hard white fat surrounding beef and calf kidneys; used in making pastries and forcemeats. May have to be ordered from your butcher; we recommend using only fresh suet. A 300g piece of fresh suet makes about 2 cups (150g) grated fresh suet.

SUGAR: we used coarse granulated table sugar, also known as crystal sugar unless otherwise specified.

Brown: a soft, fine granulated sugar containing molasses to give its characteristic colour.

TABASCO: brand name of an American-made hot sauce made from vinegar, red peppers and salt.

TACO SEASONING MIX: a packaged Mexican seasoning mix made from oregano, cumin, chillies and various other spices.

TAGINE: both the name for a North African stew and the casserole dish it is cooked in.

TAHINI: a rich buttery paste made from crushed sesame seeds.

TAMARIND PULP CONCENTRATE: a thick, purple-black paste made from the acidic, sweet-tart tasting fruit of the tamarind tree.

TOMATO:

Cherry: also known as Tiny Tim or Tom Thumb tomatoes, small and round.

Egg: also called plum or Roma, these are smallish, oval-shaped tomatoes much used in Italian cooking or salads.

Paste: a concentrated tomato puree used to flavour soups, stews, sauces and casseroles.

Sauce: tomato ketchup; a universally popular, spicy-flavoured condiment.

Sun-dried: dehydrated tomatoes. We use sun-dried tomatoes packaged in oil unless otherwise specified.

Sun-dried tomato paste: a thick paste made from sun-dried tomatoes, oil, vinegar and herbs.

TORTILLA: thin, round unleavened bread; can be made at home or purchased, frozen or vacuum-packed. Two kinds are available, one made from corn and the other wheat flour.

TOSTADA: a flour tortilla, fried until crisp.

VINEGAR:

Balsamic: authentic only from the province of Modena, Italy; made from a regional wine of white Trebbiano grapes specially processed then aged in antique wooden casks to give its exquisite pungent flavour.

Brown malt: made from fermented malt and beech shavings.

Cider: made from fermented apples.

Rice wine: made from fermented rice.

White wine: made from white wine.

WASABI: an Asian horseradish used to make a fiery sauce traditionally served with Japanese raw-fish dishes.

WATERCRESS: small, crisp, deep-green, rounded leaves having a slightly bitter, peppery flavour. Good in salads, soups and sandwiches.

WORCESTERSHIRE SAUCE: a thin, dark-brown spicy sauce used as a seasoning for meat, gravies and cocktails and as a condiment.

YEAST: a 7g (1/4oz) sachet of dried yeast (2 teaspoons) is equal to 15g (1/2oz) compressed yeast.

ZUCCHINI: courgette.

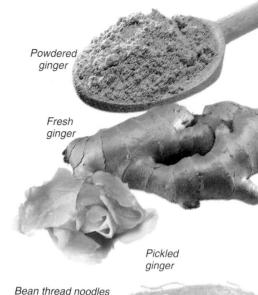

Powdered ginger

Fresh ginger

Pickled ginger

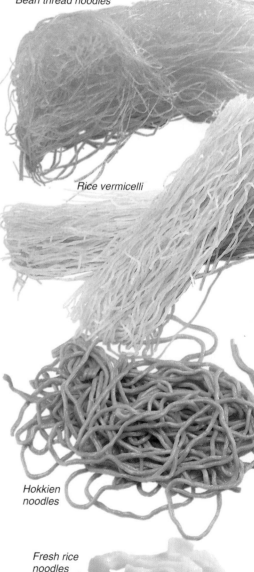

Bean thread noodles

Rice vermicelli

Hokkien noodles

Kaffir lime leaves

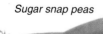

Sugar snap peas

Snow peas

Fresh rice noodles

Index

QUICK CONVERSION GUIDE

Wherever you live in the world you can use our recipes with the help of our easy-to -follow conversions for all your cooking needs. These conversions are approximate only. The difference between the exact and approximate conversion of liquid and dry measures amounts to only a teaspoon or two, and will not make any difference to your cooking results.

MEASURING EQUIPMENT

The difference between measuring cups internationally is minimal within 2 or 3 teaspoons' difference. (For the record, 1 Australian metric measuring cup will hold approximately 250ml.) The most accurate way of measuring dry ingredients is to weigh them. When measuring liquids use a clear glass or plastic jug with the metric markings.

If you would like the measuring cups and spoons as used in our Test Kitchen, turn to page 128 for details and order coupon. In this book we use metric measuring cups and spoons approved by Standards Australia.

- a graduated set of four cups for measuring dry ingredients; the sizes are marked on the cups.
- a graduated set of four spoons for measuring dry and liquid ingredients; the amounts are marked on the spoons.
- 1 TEASPOON: 5ml
- 1 TABLESPOON:20ml.

NOTE: NZ, CANADA, USA AND UK ALL USE 15ml TABLESPOONS.
ALL CUP AND SPOON MEASUREMENTS ARE LEVEL.

DRY MEASURES

METRIC	IMPERIAL
15g	1/2oz
30g	1oz
60g	2oz
90g	3oz
125g	4oz (1/4lb)
155g	5oz
185g	6oz
220g	7oz
250g	8oz (1/2lb)
280g	9oz
315g	10oz
345g	11oz
375g	12oz (3/4lb)
410g	13oz
440g	14oz
470g	15oz
500g	16oz (1lb)
750g	24oz (11/2lb)
1kg	32oz (2lb)

LIQUID MEASURES

METRIC	IMPERIAL
30ml	1 fluid oz
60ml	2 fluid oz
100ml	3 fluid oz
125ml	4 fluid oz
150ml	5 fluid oz (1/4 pint/1 gill)
190ml	6 fluid oz
250ml	8 fluid oz
300ml	10 fluid oz (1/2 pint)
500ml	16 fluid oz
600ml	20 fluid oz (1 pint)
1000ml (1 litre)	13/4 pints

WE USE LARGE EGGS
WITH AN AVERAGE
WEIGHT OF 60g

HELPFUL MEASURES

METRIC	IMPERIAL
3mm	1/8in
6mm	1/4in
1cm	1/2in
2cm	3/4in
2.5cm	1in
5cm	2in
6cm	21/2in
8cm	3in
10cm	4in
13cm	5in
15cm	6in
18cm	7in
20cm	8in
23cm	9in
25cm	10in
28cm	11in
30cm	12in (1ft)

HOW TO MEASURE

When using the graduated metric measuring cups, it is important to shake the dry ingredients loosely into the required cup. Do not tap the cup on the bench, or pack the ingredients into the cup unless otherwise directed. Level top of cup with knife. When using graduated metric measuring spoons, level top of spoon with knife. When measuring liquids in the jug, place jug on flat surface, check for accuracy at eye level.

OVEN TEMPERATURES

These oven temperatures are only a guide; we've given you the lower degree of heat. Always check the manufacturer's manual.

	C° (Celsius)	F° (Fahrenheit)	Gas Mark
Very slow	120	250	1
Slow	150	300	2
Moderately slow	160	325	3
Moderate	180 - 190	350 - 375	4
Moderately hot	200 - 210	400 - 425	5
Hot	220 - 230	450 - 475	6
Very hot	240 - 250	500 - 525	7

TWO GREAT OFFERS FROM THE AWW HOME LIBRARY

Here's the perfect way to keep your Home Library books in order, clean and within easy reach. More than a dozen books fit into this smart silver grey vinyl folder. PRICE: Australia $11.95; elsewhere $21.95; prices include postage and handling. To order your holder, see the details below.

All recipes in the AWW Home Library are created using Australia's unique system of metric cups and spoons. While it is relatively easy for overseas readers to make any minor conversions required, it is easier still to own this durable set of Australian cups and spoons (photographed). PRICE : Australia: $5.95; New Zealand: $A8.00; elsewhere: $A9.95; prices include postage & handling.
This offer is available in all countries.

TO ORDER YOUR METRIC MEASURING SET OR BOOK HOLDER:

PHONE: Have your credit card details ready. Sydney: (02) 9260 0035; **elsewhere in Australia:** 1800 252 515 (free call, Mon-Fri, 8.30am-5.30pm) or FAX your order to (02) 9267 4363 or MAIL your order by photocopying or cutting out and completing the coupon below.

PAYMENT: **Australian residents:** We accept the credit cards listed, money orders and cheques. **Overseas residents:** We accept the credit cards listed, drafts in $A drawn on an Australian bank, also English, New Zealand and U.S. cheques in the currency of the country of issue.
Credit card charges are at the exchange rate current at the time of payment.

Please photocopy and complete coupon and fax or send to:
AWW Home Library Reader Offer, ACP Direct, PO Box 7036, Sydney 1028.